D0792555

MINISTER'S MANUAL

MINISTER'S MANUAL

Compiled and Edited by
WILLIAM E. PICKTHORN

Volume 1
SERVICES FOR SPECIAL OCCASIONS

Volume 2
SERVICES FOR WEDDINGS
AND FUNERALS

Volume 3
SERVICES FOR MINISTERS
AND WORKERS

MINISTER'S MANUAL

Compiled and Edited by
WILLIAM E. PICKTHORN

Volume 1
SERVICES FOR SPECIAL OCCASIONS

GOSPEL PUBLISHING HOUSE
Springfield, Missouri 65802

02-0547

Library of Congress
Catalog Card No. 65-13222
ISBN 0-88243-547-7

PREFACE

"It hardly needs to be said that set forms of devotion are uncongenial to those who practice a simple mode of worship and who stress spiritual liberty in prayer and preaching.

"Yet, while recognizing this fact it still remains true that there are special occasions where an appointed order is necessary for a well-conducted service. And if this is so, why be content with forms that are crude or badly prepared? Jesus in the Scripture portion known as the Lord's Prayer instructed the disciples: 'When ye pray, say . . .' The prophet Hosea once said to his countrymen: 'Take with you words, and turn to the Lord, and say to Him . . .' Hosea 14:2.

"There need be no morbid fear of lifeless ritual. As long as the spiritual vitality of the church is maintained the use of necessary forms will never become merely formal."

So wrote Myer Pearlman in the foreword to the first minister's manual produced by the Gospel Publishing House, *The Minister's Service Book*. These words, so true then, are just as true today. Every service must be ordered in some way, but no service need be lifeless and mechanical. The minister, guided by the Spirit, can select ceremonies which he feels contain the touch of the Spirit and which are appropriate to an occasion. Under the leading of the Spirit, he may adapt ceremonies to take into account unique circumstances. Perhaps he may even accept the challenge to write a ceremony of his own! Let this manual be a servant, not a master.

WILLIAM E. PICKTHORN
Christian Center
Palo Alto, California

ACKNOWLEDGMENTS

Credit for suggestions as to what should go into this volume is due to a great many ministers whose names are not in this book. They are men who wrote to say what they would like to see included even though they did not, themselves, submit forms for publication.

Credit for inspiration is due to a great many manuals published over a period of almost 90 years and by many different religious denominations. It is not thought that any of the material in this book has been lifted directly from any other manual. Forms sent by ministers who have contributed to the contents of this book were checked against the available manuals to avoid unintentional infringement of copyright. In instances where there were gaps in the materials received, the editor of this manual made outline notes on procedures detailed in various manuals, and, during a period of more than a year, revised the notes three or more times without reference to original sources so that the materials would become more and more his own. If there are forms in this manual resembling those of any other published book it is through sheer coincidence that they possess such similarity.

Deep appreciation and fervent thanks are both extended to those who, through the years, have compiled such manuals. May their inspiration continue to affect others as it has me.

W.E.P.

CONTENTS

GOD'S WORD OF COMFORT

THE FAITH

THE CHURCH

WORSHIP

DEDICATION OF CHILDREN

WATER BAPTISM

RECEPTION OF MEMBERS

COMMUNION SERVICE

God's Word of Comfort

THE SICK

"I am the Lord that healeth thee." (Ex. 15:26)

"My presence shall go with thee, and I will give thee rest." (Ex. 33:14)

"I will both lay me down in peace, and sleep: for thou, Lord, only makest me dwell in safety." (Ps. 4:8)

"The Lord is my shepherd; I shall not want. He maketh me to lie down in green pastures: he leadeth me beside the still waters. He restoreth my soul: he leadeth me in the paths of righteousness for his name's sake. Yea, though I walk through the valley of the shadow of death, I will fear no evil: for thou art with me; thy rod and thy staff they comfort me. Thou preparest a table before me in the presence of mine enemies: thou anointest my head with oil; my cup runneth over. Surely goodness and mercy shall follow me all the days of my life: and I will dwell in the house of the Lord for ever." (Ps. 23)

"The Lord is my light and my salvation; whom shall I fear? The Lord is the strength of my life; of whom shall I be afraid? When the wicked, even mine enemies and my foes, came upon me to eat up my flesh, they stumbled and fell. Though an host should encamp against me, my heart shall not fear: though war should rise against me, in this will I be confident. One thing have I desired of the Lord, that will I seek after; that I may dwell in the house of the Lord all the days of my life, to behold the beauty of the Lord, and to inquire in his temple. For in the time of trouble he shall hide me in his pavilion: in the secret of his tabernacle shall he hide me; he shall set me up upon a rock. And now shall mine head be lifted up above mine enemies round about me: therefore will I offer in his tabernacle sacrifices of joy; I will sing, yea, I will sing praises unto the Lord." (Ps. 27:1-6)

"God is our refuge and strength, a very present help in the time of trouble." (Ps. 46:1)

"He that dwelleth in the secret place of the most High shall abide under the shadow of the Almighty." (Ps. 91:1)

"He shall give his angels charge over thee, to keep thee in all thy ways." (Ps. 91:11)

"He shall call upon me, and I will answer him: I will be with him in trouble; I will deliver him, and honour him." (Ps. 91:15)

"Bless the Lord, O my soul: and all that is within me, bless his holy name. Who forgiveth all thine iniquities; who healeth all thy diseases." (Ps. 103:1, 3)

"He maketh the storm a calm, so that the waves thereof are still. Then are they glad because they be quiet; so he bringeth them unto their desired haven." (Ps. 107:29, 30)

"I will lift up mine eyes unto the hills, from whence cometh my help. My help cometh from the

Lord, which made heaven and earth. He will not suffer thy foot to be moved: he that keepeth thee will not slumber. Behold, he that keepeth Israel shall neither slumber nor sleep. The Lord is thy keeper: the Lord is thy shade upon thy right hand. The sun shall not smite thee by day, nor the moon by night. The Lord shall preserve thee from all evil: he shall preserve thy soul. The Lord shall preserve thy going out and thy coming in from this time forth, and even for evermore." (Ps. 121)

"In quietness and in confidence shall be your strength." (Isa. 30:15)

"They that wait upon the Lord shall renew their strength; they shall mount up with wings as eagles; they shall run, and not be weary; they shall walk, and not faint." (Isa. 40:31)

"Behold, I am the Lord, the God of all flesh: is there any thing too hard for me?" (Jer. 32:27)

"I will lay sinews upon you, and will bring up flesh upon you, and cover you with skin, and put breath in you, and ye shall live; and ye shall know that I am the Lord." (Ezek. 37:6)

"Jesus saith unto him, I will come and heal him. The centurion answered and said, Lord, I am not worthy that thou shouldest come under my roof: but speak the word only, and my servant shall be healed." (Matt. 8:7, 8)

"Jesus ... said unto them, They that be whole need not a physician, but they that are sick. But go

3

ye and learn what that meaneth, I will have mercy, and not sacrifice: for I am not come to call the righteous, but sinners to repentance."

(Matt. 9:12, 13)

"Lo, I am with you alway, even unto the end of the world." (Matt. 28:20)

"Peace I leave with you, my peace I give unto you: not as the world giveth, give I unto you. Let not your heart be troubled, neither let it be afraid."

(John 14:27)

"Be careful for nothing; but in every thing by prayer and supplication with thanksgiving let your requests be made known unto God. And the peace of God which passeth all understanding, shall keep your hearts and minds through Christ Jesus."

(Phil. 4:6, 7)

"This is the confidence that we have in him, that, if we ask any thing according to his will, he heareth us: and if we know that he hear us, whatsoever we ask, we know that we have the petitions that we desired of him." (1 John 5:14, 15)

"Beloved, I wish above all things that thou mayest prosper and be in health, even as thy soul prospereth." (3 John 2)

THE TROUBLED

"Behold, happy is the man whom God correcteth: therefore despise not thou the chastening of the Almighty: for he maketh sore, and bindeth up: he woundeth, and his hands make whole. He shall deliver thee in six troubles: yea, in seven there shall no evil touch thee. In famine he shall redeem thee from death: and in war from the power of the sword. Thou shalt be hid from the scourge of the tongue: neither shalt thou be afraid of destruction when it cometh. At destruction and famine thou shalt laugh: neither shalt thou be afraid of the beast of the earth. For thou shalt be in league with the stones of the field: and the beasts of the field shall be at peace with thee. And thou shalt know that thy tabernacle shall be in peace; and thou shalt visit thy habitation, and shalt not sin. Thou shalt know also that thy seed shall be great, and thine offspring as the grass of the earth. Thou shalt come to thy grave in a full age, like as a shock of corn cometh in in his season." (Job 5:17-26)

"Be still, and know that I am God: I will be exalted among the heathen, I will be exalted in the earth." (Ps. 46:10)

"He that dwelleth in the secret place of the most High shall abide under the shadow of the Almighty. I will say of the Lord, He is my refuge and my fortress: my God; in him will I trust. Surely he shall deliver thee from the snare of the fowler, and from the noisome pestilence. He shall cover thee with his feathers, and under his wings shalt thou trust: his truth shall be thy shield and buckler. Thou shalt not be afraid for the terror by night; nor for the arrow that flieth by day; nor for the destruction that wasteth at noonday. A thousand shall fall at thy side, and ten thousand at thy right hand; but it shall not come nigh thee. Only with thine eyes shalt thou behold and see the reward of the wicked." (Ps. 91:1-8)

"Blessed is the man whom thou chastenest, O Lord, and teachest him out of thy law; that thou mayest give him rest from the days of adversity, until the pit be digged for the wicked. For the Lord will not cast off his people, neither will he forsake his inheritance." (Ps. 94:12-14)

"My son, despise not the chastening of the Lord; neither be weary of his correction: for whom the Lord loveth he correcteth; even as a father the son in whom he delighteth." (Prov. 3:11, 12)

"Behold, God is my salvation; I will trust, and not be afraid: for the Lord Jehovah is my strength and my song; he also is become my salvation." (Isa. 12:2)

"Thou wilt keep him in perfect peace, whose mind is stayed on thee: because he trusteth in thee." (Isa. 26:3)

"Let not your heart be troubled: ye believe in God, believe also in me." (John 14:1)

6

"And we know that all things work together for good to them that love God, to them who are the called according to his purpose." (Rom. 8:28)

"There hath no temptation taken you but such as is common to man: but God is faithful, who will not suffer you to be tempted above that ye are able; but will with the temptation also make a way to escape, that ye may be able to bear it."

(1 Cor. 10:13)

"Blessed be God, even the Father of our Lord Jesus Christ, the Father of mercies, and the God of all comfort; who comforteth us in all our tribulation, that we may be able to comfort them which are in any trouble, by the comfort wherewith we ourselves are comforted of God. For as the sufferings of Christ abound in us, so our consolation also aboundeth by Christ. And whether we be afflicted, it is for your consolation and salvation, which is effectual in the enduring of the same sufferings which we also suffer: or whether we be comforted, it is for your consolation and salvation. And our hope of you is stedfast, knowing, that as ye are partakers of the sufferings, so shall ye be also of the consolation."

(2 Cor. 1:3-7)

"For our light affliction, which is but for a moment, worketh for us a far more exceeding and eternal weight of glory; while we look not at the things which are seen, but at the things which are not seen: for the things which are seen are temporal; but the things which are not seen are eternal."

(2 Cor. 4:17, 18)

"For it is better, if the will of God be so, that ye suffer for well doing, than for evil doing."

(1 Peter 3:17)

"Beloved, think it not strange concerning the fiery trial which is to try you, as though some strange thing happened unto you: but rejoice, inasmuch as ye are partakers of Christ's sufferings; that, when his glory shall be revealed, ye may be glad also with exceeding joy." (1 Peter 4:12, 13)

THE TEMPTED

"Watch ye therefore, and pray always, that ye may be accounted worthy to escape all these things that shall come to pass, and to stand before the Son of man." (Luke 21:36)

"There hath no temptation taken you but such as is common to man: but God is faithful, who will not suffer you to be tempted above that ye are able; but will with the temptation also make a way to escape, that ye may be able to bear it." (1 Cor. 10:13)

"Finally, my brethren, be strong in the Lord, and in the power of his might. Put on the whole armour of God, that ye may be able to stand against the wiles of the devil." (Eph. 6:10, 11)

"My brethren, count it all joy when ye fall into divers temptations; knowing this, that the trying of your faith worketh patience." (James 1:2, 3)

"Blessed is the man that endureth temptation: for when he is tried, he shall receive the crown of life, which the Lord hath promised to them that love him." (James 1:12)

"Let no man say when he is tempted, I am tempted of God: for God cannot be tempted with evil, neither tempteth he any man: but every man is tempted, when he is drawn away of his own lust, and enticed." (James 1:13, 14)

"Blessed be the God and Father of our Lord Jesus Christ, which according to his abundant mercy hath begotten us again unto a lively hope by the resurrection of Jesus Christ from the dead, to an inheritance incorruptible, and undefiled, and that fadeth not away, reserved in heaven for you, who are kept by the power of God through faith unto salvation ready to be revealed in the last time. Wherein ye greatly rejoice, though now for a season, if need be, ye are in heaviness through manifold temptations: that the trial of your faith, being much more precious than of gold that perisheth, though it be tried with fire, might be found unto praise and honour and glory at the appearing of Jesus Christ." (1 Peter 1:3-7)

THE BEREAVED

"And he said, The Lord is my rock, and my fortress, and my deliverer; the God of my rock; in him will I trust: he is my shield, and the horn of my salvation, my high tower, and my refuge, my saviour; thou savest me from violence."

(2 Sam. 22:2, 3)

"God is our refuge and strength, a very present help in trouble." (Ps. 46:1)

"He that dwelleth in the secret place of the most High shall abide under the shadow of the Almighty. I will say of the Lord, He is my refuge and my fortress: my God; in him will I trust. Surely he shall deliver thee from the snare of the fowler, and from the noisome pestilence. He shall cover thee with his feathers, and under his wings shalt thou trust: his truth shall be thy shield and buckler." (Ps. 91:1-4)

"When thou passest through the waters, I will be with thee; and through the rivers, they shall not overflow thee: when thou walkest through the fire, thou shalt not be burned; neither shall the flame kindle upon thee." (Isa. 43:2)

"Come unto me, all ye that labour and are heavy laden, and I will give you rest. Take my yoke upon you, and learn of me; for I am meek and lowly in heart: and ye shall find rest unto your souls. For my yoke is easy, and my burden is light."

(Matt. 11:28-30)

"And we know that all things work together for good to them that love God, to them who are the called according to his purpose. For whom he did foreknow, he also did predestinate to be conformed to the image of his Son, that he might be the first-born among many brethren. Moreover, whom he did predestinate, them he also called: and whom he called, them he also justified: and whom he justified, them he also glorified. What shall we then say to these things? If God be for us, who can be against us? He that spared not his own Son, but delivered him up for us all, how shall he not with him also freely give us all things? Who shall lay anything to the charge of God's elect? It is God that justi-fieth. Who is he that condemneth? It is Christ that died, yea rather, that is risen again, who is even at the right hand of God, who also maketh inter-cession for us. Who shall separate us from the love of Christ? shall tribulation, or distress, or persecu-tion, or famine, or nakedness, or peril, or sword? As it is written, For thy sake we are killed all the day long; we are accounted as sheep for the slaughter. Nay, in all these things we are more than conquerors through him that loved us. For I am persuaded, that neither death, nor life, nor angels, nor principalities, nor powers, nor things present, nor things to come, nor height, nor depth, nor any other creature, shall be able to separate us from the love of God, which is in Christ Jesus our Lord." (Rom. 8:28-39)

"For our light affliction, which is but for a moment, worketh for us a far more exceeding and eternal weight of glory; while we look not at the things which are seen, but at the things which are not seen: for the things which are seen are temporal; but the things which are not seen are eternal."

(2 Cor. 4:17, 18)

"And ye have forgotten the exhortation which speaketh unto you as unto children, My son, despise not thou the chastening of the Lord, nor faint when thou art rebuked of him: for whom the Lord loveth he chasteneth, and scourgeth every son whom he receiveth. If ye endure chastening, God dealeth with you as with sons; for what son is he whom the father chasteneth not? But if ye be without chastisement, whereof all are partakers, then are ye bastards, and not sons. Furthermore we have had fathers of our flesh which corrected us, and we gave them reverence: shall we not much rather be in subjection unto the Father of spirits, and live? For they verily for a few days chastened us after their own pleasure; but he for our profit, that we might be partakers of his holiness. Now no chastening for the present seemeth to be joyous, but grievous: nevertheless afterward it yieldeth the peaceable fruit of righteousness unto them which are exercised thereby."

(Heb. 12:5-11)

CONFESSION

"I have sinned; what shall I do unto thee, O thou preserver of men? why hast thou set me as a mark against thee, so that I am a burden to myself? And why dost thou not pardon my transgression, and take away mine iniquity? for now shall I sleep in the dust; and thou shalt seek me in the morning, but I shall not be." (Job 7:20,21)

"Have mercy upon me, O God, according to thy lovingkindness: according unto the multitude of thy tender mercies blot out my transgressions. For I acknowledge my transgressions: and my sin is ever before me. Against thee, thee only, have I sinned, and done this evil in thy sight: that thou mightest be justified when thou speakest, and be clear when thou judgest." (Ps. 51:1, 3, 4)

"For our transgressions are multiplied before thee, and our sins testify against us: for our transgressions are with us; and as for our iniquities, we know them; in transgressing and lying against the Lord, and departing away from our God, speaking oppression and revolt, conceiving and uttering from the heart words of falsehood. And judgment is turned away backward, and justice standeth afar off: for truth is fallen in the street, and equity cannot enter. Yea, truth faileth; and he that departeth from evil maketh himself a prey: and the Lord saw it, and it displeased him that there was no judgment." (Isa. 59:12-15)

"We have sinned, and have committed iniquity, and have done wickedly, and have rebelled, even by departing from thy precepts and from thy judgments: neither have we hearkened unto thy servants the prophets, which spake in thy name to our kings, our princes, and our fathers, and to all the people of the land. O Lord, righteousness belongeth unto thee, but unto us confusion of faces, as at this day; to the men of Judah, and to the inhabitants of Jerusalem, and unto all Israel, that are near, and that are far off, through all the countries whither thou hast driven them, because of their trespass that they have trespassed against thee. O Lord, to us belongeth confusion of face, to our kings, to our princes, and to our fathers, because we have sinned against thee. To the Lord our God belong mercies and forgivenesses, though we have rebelled against him; neither have we obeyed the voice of the Lord our God, to walk in his laws, which he set before us by his servants the prophets." (Dan. 9:5-10)

"Whosoever therefore shall confess me before men, him will I confess also before my Father which is in heaven." (Matt. 10:32)

"That if thou shalt confess with thy mouth the Lord Jesus, and shalt believe in thine heart that God hath raised him from the dead, thou shalt be saved. For with the heart man believeth unto righteousness; and with the mouth confession is made unto salvation." (Rom. 10:9, 10)

"If we confess our sins, he is faithful and just to forgive us our sins, and to cleanse us from all unrighteousness." (1 John 1:9)

"They are of the world: therefore speak they of the world, and the world heareth them."

(1 John 4:5)

FAITH

"And he said unto her, Daughter, thy faith hath made thee whole; go in peace, and be whole of thy plague." (Mark 5:34)

"And he said to the woman, Thy faith hath saved thee; go in peace." (Luke 7:50)

"Therefore we conclude that a man is justified by faith without the deeds of the law." (Rom. 3:28)

"Therefore being justified by faith, we have peace with God through our Lord Jesus Christ: by whom also we have access by faith into this grace wherein we stand, and rejoice in the hope of the glory of God." (Rom. 5:1, 2)

"So then faith cometh by hearing, and hearing by the word of God." (Rom. 10:17)

"Now faith is the substance of things hoped for, the evidence of things not seen. For by it the elders obtained a good report. Through faith we understand that the worlds were framed by the word of God, so that things which are seen were not made of things which do appear." (Heb. 11:1-3)

"And this is his commandment, That we should believe on the name of his Son Jesus Christ, and love one another, as he gave us commandment." (1 John 3:23)

The Faith

"Give ear, O ye heavens, and I will speak; and hear, O earth, the words of my mouth. My doctrine shall drop as the rain, my speech shall distil as the dew, as the small rain upon the tender herb, and as the showers upon the grass: because I will publish the name of the Lord: ascribe ye greatness unto our God."   (Deut. 32:1-3)

"Jesus answered them, and said, My doctrine is not mine, but his that sent me. If any man will do his will, he shall know of the doctrine, whether it be of God, or whether I speak of myself."
                                        (John 7:16, 17)

"But God be thanked, that ye were the servants of sin, but ye have obeyed from the heart that form of doctrine which was delivered you."   (Rom. 6:17)

"There is one body, and one Spirit, even as ye are called in one hope of your calling; one Lord, one faith, one baptism, one God and Father of all, who is above all, and through all, and in you all."
                                        (Eph. 4:4-6)

"If thou put the brethren in remembrance of these things, thou shalt be a good minister of Jesus Christ, nourished up in the words of faith and of good doctrine, whereunto thou hast attained."
                                        (1 Tim. 4:6)

"All scripture is given by inspiration of God, and is profitable for doctrine, for reproof, for correction, for instruction in righteousness: that the man of God may be perfect, throughly furnished unto all good works."　　　(2 Tim. 3:16, 17)

"I have fought a good fight, I have finished my course, I have kept the faith."　　　(2 Tim. 4:7)

"But speak thou the things which become sound doctrine."　　　(Titus 2:1)

"Simon Peter, a servant and an apostle of Jesus Christ, to them that have obtained like precious faith with us through the righteousness of God and our Saviour Jesus Christ: grace and peace be multiplied unto you through the knowledge of God and of Jesus our Lord."　　　(2 Peter 1:1, 2)

"But, beloved, remember ye the words which were spoken before of the apostles of our Lord Jesus Christ; how that they told you there should be mockers in the last time, who should walk after their own ungodly lusts. These be they who separate themselves, sensual, having not the Spirit. But ye, beloved, building up yourselves on your most holy faith, praying in the Holy Ghost, keep yourselves in the love of God, looking for the mercy of our Lord Jesus Christ unto eternal life."　　　(Jude 17-21)

GENERAL COUNCIL OF THE ASSEMBLIES OF GOD

STATEMENT OF FUNDAMENTAL TRUTHS

ARTICLE V—CONSTITUTION

(Revised 1969 General Council)

The Bible is our all-sufficient rule for faith and practice. This Statement of Fundamental Truths is intended simply as a basis of fellowship among us (i.e., that we all speak the same thing, 1 Cor. 1:10; Acts 2:42). The phraseology employed in this Statement is not inspired or contended for, but the truth set forth is held to be essential to a full-gospel ministry. No claim is made that it contains all Biblical truth, only that it covers our need as to these fundamental doctrines.

1. THE SCRIPTURES INSPIRED

The Scriptures, both the Old and New Testaments, are verbally inspired of God and are the revelation of God to man, the infallible, authoritative rule of faith and conduct (2 Tim. 3:15-17; 1 Thess. 2:13; 2 Peter 1:21).

2. THE ONE TRUE GOD

The one true God has revealed Himself as the eternally self-existent "I AM," the Creator of heaven and earth and the Redeemer of mankind. He has further revealed Himself as embodying the principles of relationship and association as Father, Son and Holy Ghost (Deut. 6:4; Isa. 43:10, 11; Matt. 28:19; Luke 3:22).

21

THE ADORABLE GODHEAD

(a) Terms Defined

The terms "Trinity" and "persons" as related to the Godhead, while not found in the Scriptures, are words in harmony with Scripture, whereby we may convey to others our immediate understanding of the doctrine of Christ respecting the Being of God, as distinguished from "gods many and lords many." We therefore may speak with propriety of the Lord our God, who is One Lord, as a trinity or as one Being of three persons, and still be absolutely scriptural (examples, Matt. 28:19; 2 Cor. 13:14; John 14:16, 17).

(b) Distinction and Relationship in the Godhead

Christ taught a distinction of Persons in the Godhead which He expressed in specific terms of relationship, as Father, Son, and Holy Ghost, but that this distinction and relationship, as to its mode is *inscrutable* and *incomprehensible,* because *unexplained.* Luke 1:35; 1 Cor. 1:24; Matt. 11:25-27; 28:19; 2 Cor. 13:14; 1 John 1:3, 4.

(c) Unity of the One Being of Father, Son and Holy Ghost

Accordingly, therefore, there is *that* in the Son which constitutes Him *the Son* and not the Father; and there is *that* in the Holy Ghost which constitutes Him *the Holy Ghost* and not either the Father or the Son. Wherefore the Father is the Begetter, the Son is the Begotten, and the Holy Ghost is the one proceeding from the Father and the Son. Therefore, because these three persons in the Godhead are in a state of unity, there is but one Lord God Almighty and His name one. John 1:18; 15:26; 17:11, 21; Zech. 14:9.

(d) *Identity and Cooperation in the Godhead*

The Father, the Son and the Holy Ghost are never *identical* as to *Person*; nor *confused* as to *relation*; nor *divided* in respect to the Godhead; nor *opposed* as to *cooperation*. The Son is *in* the Father and the Father is *in* the Son as to relationship. The Son is *with* the Father and the Father is *with* the Son, as to fellowship. The Father is not *from* the Son, but the Son is *from* the Father, as to authority. The Holy Ghost is *from* the Father and the Son proceeding, as to nature, relationship, cooperation and authority. Hence, neither Person in the Godhead either exists or works separately or independently of the others. John 5:17-30, 32, 37; John 8:17, 18.

(e) *The Title, Lord Jesus Christ*

The appellation, "Lord Jesus Christ," is a proper name. It is never applied, in the New Testament, either to the Father or to the Holy Ghost. It therefore belongs exclusively to the *Son of God*. Rom. 1:1-3, 7; 2 John 3.

(f) *The Lord Jesus Christ, God with Us*

The Lord Jesus Christ, as to His divine and eternal nature, is the proper and only Begotten of the Father, but as to His human nature, He is the proper Son of Man. He is, therefore, acknowledged

to be both God and man; who because He is God
and man, is "Immanuel," God with us. Matt. 1:23;
1 John 4:2, 10, 14; Rev. 1:13, 17.

(g) *The Title, Son of God*

Since the name "Immanuel" embraces both God
and man in the one Person, our Lord Jesus Christ,
it follows that the title, Son of God, describes His
proper deity, and the title Son of Man, His proper
humanity. Therefore, the title, Son of God, belongs
to the *order of eternity,* and the title, Son of Man,
to the *order of time.* Matt. 1:21-23; 2 John 3; 1 John
3:8; Heb. 7:3; 1:1-13.

(h) *Transgression of the Doctrine of Christ*

Wherefore, it is a transgression of the Doctrine
of Christ to say that Jesus Christ derived the title, Son
of God, solely from the fact of the incarnation, or
because of His relation to the economy of redemption. Therefore, to deny that the Father is a real
and eternal Father, and that the Son is a real and
eternal Son, is a denial of the distinction and relationship in the Being of God; a denial of the Father
and the Son; and a displacement of the truth that
Jesus Christ is come in the flesh. 2 John 9; John
1:1, 2, 14, 18, 29, 49; 1 John 2:22, 23; 4:1-5; Heb.
12:2.

(i) *Exaltation of Jesus Christ as Lord*

The Son of God, our Lord Jesus Christ, having
by Himself purged our sins, sat down on the right
hand of the Majesty on high; angels and principalities and powers having been made subject unto Him.

And having been made both Lord and Christ, He sent the Holy Ghost that we, in the name of Jesus, might bow our knees and confess that Jesus Christ is Lord to the glory of God the Father until the end, when the Son shall become subject to the Father that God may be all in all. Heb. 1:3; 1 Peter 3:22; Acts 2:32-36; Rom. 14:11; 1 Cor. 15:24-28.

(j) *Equal Honor to the Father and to the Son*

Wherefore, since the Father has delivered all judgment unto the Son, it is not only the *express duty* of all in heaven and on earth to bow the knee, but it is an *unspeakable* joy in the Holy Ghost to ascribe unto the Son all the attributes of Deity, and to give Him all the honor and the glory contained in all the names and titles of the Godhead (except those which express relationship. See paragraphs b, c, and d), and thus honor the Son even as we honor the Father. John 5:22, 23; 1 Peter 1:8; Rev. 5:6-14; Phil. 2:8, 9; Rev. 7:9, 10; 4:8-11.

3. THE DEITY OF THE LORD JESUS CHRIST

The Lord Jesus Christ is the eternal Son of God. The Scriptures declare:

(a) His virgin birth (Matt. 1:23; Luke 1:31, 35).

(b) His sinless life (Heb. 7:26; 1 Peter 2:22)

(c) His miracles (Acts 2:22; 10:38).

(d) His substitutionary work on the cross (1 Cor. 15:3; 2 Cor. 5:21).

(e) His bodily resurrection from the dead (Matt. 28:6; Luke 24:39; 1 Cor. 15:4).

(f) His exaltation to the right hand of God (Acts 1:9, 11; 2:33; Phil. 2:9-11; Heb. 1-3).

4. THE FALL OF MAN

Man was created good and upright; for God said, "Let us make man in our image, after our likeness." However, man by voluntary trangression fell and thereby incurred not only physical death but also spiritual death, which is separation from God (Gen. 1:26, 27; 2:17; 3:6; Rom. 5:12-19).

5: THE SALVATION OF MAN

Man's only hope of redemption is through the shed blood of Jesus Christ the Son of God.

(a) Conditions to Salvation

Salvation is received repentance toward God and faith toward the Lord Jesus Christ. By the washing of regeneration and renewing of the Holy Ghost, being justified by grace through faith, man becomes an heir of God, according to the hope of eternal life (Luke 24:47; John 3:3; Rom. 10:13-15; Eph. 2:8; Titus 2:11; 3:5-7).

(b) The Evidences of Salvation

The inward evidence of salvation is the direct witness of the Spirit (Romans 8:16). The outward evidence to all men is a life of righteousness and true holiness (Eph. 4:24; Titus 2:12).

6. ORDINANCES OF THE CHURCH

(a) Baptism in Water

The ordinance of baptism by immersion is commanded in the Scriptures. All who repent and believe on Christ as Saviour and Lord are to be baptized. Thus they declare to the world that they have died with Christ and that they also have been raised with Him to walk in newness of life. (Matt. 28:19; Mark 16:16; Acts 10:47, 48; Rom. 6:4).

(b) Holy Communion

The Lord's Supper, consisting of the elements—bread and the fruit of the vine—is the symbol expressing our sharing the divine nature of our Lord Jesus Christ (2 Peter 1:4) ; a memorial of His suffering and death (1 Cor. 11:26) ; and a prophecy of His second coming (1 Cor. 11:26) ; and is enjoined on all believers "till He come!"

7. THE BAPTISM IN THE HOLY GHOST

All believers are entitled to and should ardently expect and earnestly seek the promise of the Father, the baptism in the Holy Ghost and fire, according to the command of our Lord Jesus Christ. This was the normal experience of all in the early Christian Church. With it comes the enduement of power for life and service, the bestowment of the gifts and their uses in the work of the ministry. (Luke 24:49; Acts 1:4, 8; 1 Cor. 12:1-31) . This experience is distinct from and subsequent to the experience of the new birth (Acts 8:12-17; 10:44-46; 11:14-16; 15:7-9) . With the baptism in the Holy Ghost come such experiences as an overflowing fullness of the Spirit (John 7:37-39; Acts 4:8) , a deepened reverence for God (Acts 2:43; Heb. 12:28) , an intensified consecration to God and dedication to His work

(Acts 2:42), and a more active love for Christ, for His Word and for the lost (Mark 16:20).

8. THE EVIDENCE OF THE BAPTISM IN THE HOLY GHOST

The baptism of believers in the Holy Ghost is witnessed by the initial physical sign of speaking with other tongues as the Spirit of God gives them utterance (Acts 2:4). The speaking in tongues in this instance is the same in essence as the gift of tongues (1 Cor. 12:4-10, 28), but different in purpose and use.

9. SANCTIFICATION

Sanctification is an act of separation from that which is evil, and of dedication unto God (Rom. 12: 1, 2; 1 Thess. 5:23; Heb. 13:12). The Scriptures teach a life of "holiness without which no man shall see the Lord" (Heb. 12:14). By the power of the Holy Ghost we are able to obey the command: "Be ye holy, for I am holy" (1 Peter 1: 15, 16).

Sanctification is realized in the believer by recognizing his identification with Christ in His death and resurrection, and by faith reckoning daily upon the fact of that union, and by offering every faculty continually to the dominion of the Holy Spirit (Rom. 6:1-11, 13; 8:1, 2, 13; Gal. 2:20; Phil. 2:12, 13; 1 Peter 1:5).

10. THE CHURCH AND ITS MISSION

The Church is the Body of Christ, the habitation of God through the Spirit, with divine appointments for the fulfillment of her great commission. Each believer, born of the Spirit, is an integral part of the General Assembly and Church of the First-born, which are written in heaven (Ephesians 1:22, 23; 2:22; Hebrews 12:23).

Since God's purpose concerning man is to seek and to save that which is lost, to be worshiped by man, and to build a body of believers in the image of His Son, the priority reason-for-being of the Assemblies of God as part of the Church is:

a. To be an agency of God for evangelizing the world (Acts 1:8; Matthew 28:19, 20; Mark 16:15, 16).

b. To be a corporate body in which man may worship God (1 Corinthians 12:13).

c. To be a channel of God's purpose to build a body of saints being perfected in the image of His Son (Ephesians 4:11-16; 1 Corinthians 12:28; 1 Corinthians 14:12).

The Assemblies of God exists expressly to give continuing emphasis to this reason-for-being in the New Testament apostolic pattern by teaching and encouraging believers to be baptized in the Holy Spirit. This experience:

a. Enables them to evangelize in the power of the Spirit with accompanying supernatural signs (Mark 16:15-20; Acts 4:29-31; Hebrews 2:3, 4).

b. Adds a necessary dimension to worshipful relationship with God (1 Corinthians 2:10-16; 1 Corinthians 12, 13, and 14).

c. Enables them to respond to the full working of the Holy Spirit in expression of fruit and gifts and ministries as in New Testament times for the edifying of the body of Christ (Galatians 5:22-26; 1 Corinthians 14:12; Ephesians 4:11, 12; 1 Corinthians 12:28; Colossians 1:29).

11. THE MINISTRY

A divinely called and scripturally ordained ministry has been provided by our Lord for the threefold purpose of leading the church in: (1) Evangelization of the world (Mark 16:15-20), (2) Worship of God (John 4:23, 24), (3) Building a body of saints being perfected in the image of His Son (Ephesians 4:11-16).

12. DIVINE HEALING

Divine healing is an integral part of the gospel. Deliverance from sickness is provided for in the atonement, and is the privilege of all believers (Isa. 53:4, 5; Matt. 8:16, 17; James 5:14-16).

13. THE BLESSED HOPE

The resurrection of those who have fallen asleep in Christ and their translation together with those who are alive and remain unto the coming of the Lord is the imminent and blessed hope of the Church (1 Thess. 4:16, 17; Rom. 8:23; Titus 2:13; 1 Cor. 15:51, 52).

14. THE MILLENNIAL REIGN OF CHRIST

The second coming of Christ includes the rapture of the saints, which is our blessed hope, followed by the visible return of Christ with His saints to reign on the earth for one thousand years (Zech. 14:5; Matt. 24:27, 30; Rev. 1:7; 19:11-14; 20:1-6). This millennial reign will bring the salvation of national Israel (Ezek. 37:21, 22; Zeph. 3:19, 20; Rom. 11:26, 27) and the establishment of universal peace (Isa. 11:6-9; Ps. 72:3-8; Micah 4:3, 4).

15. THE FINAL JUDGMENT

There will be a final judgment in which the wicked dead will be raised and judged according to their works. Whosoever is not found written in the Book of Life, together with the devil and his angels, the beast and the false prophet, will be consigned to everlasting punishment in the lake which burneth with fire and brimstone, which is the second death (Matt. 25:46; Mark 9:43-48; Rev. 19:20; 20:11-15; 21:8).

16. THE NEW HEAVENS AND THE NEW EARTH

"We, according to his promise, look for new heavens and a new earth, wherein dwelleth righteousness" (2 Peter 3:13; Rev. 21, 22).

31

THE APOSTLES' CREED

I believe in God the Father Almighty,
    Maker of heaven and earth:
And in Jesus Christ His only Son, our Lord;
    who was conceived by the Holy Ghost,
        born of the Virgin Mary,
            suffered under Pontius Pilate,
                was crucified, dead, and buried;

    He descended into hell;
    the third day He rose again from the dead:
        He ascended into heaven, and sitteth on
        the right hand of God the Father Al-
        mighty;
            from thence He shall come to judge
            the quick and the dead.

I believe in the Holy Ghost;
    the holy Catholic Church;
        the communion of saints;
            the forgiveness of sins;
                the resurrection of the body;
                and life everlasting.
                      Amen.

MY OWN CREED

I believe in the literal (verbal) inspiration and infallibility of the Bible as originally written.
  2 Peter 1:21; 3:15; 2 Tim. 3:15, 16; Acts 1:3

I believe in   Heb. 11:6
God the Father   Gal. 1:1-4
Almighty,   2 Cor. 6:17, 18; Gen. 17:1
Maker of heaven and earth: Ps. 95:6; Eph. 3:9

who gave his only begotten Son,   John 3:16
who creates a new life in believers.
Eph. 4:22-24; Col. 3:10

I believe in Jesus Christ   John 6:47
God's only begotten Son, our Lord;   John 3:18
1 John 4:9; Rom. 10:9
conceived of the Holy Spirit,   Luke 1:35;
Matt. 1:18-20
born of the Virgin Mary, Matt. 1:23; Luke 1:27
suffered under Pontius Pilate,   Matt. 27:2
was crucified, dead and buried.   Matt. 27:35
He descended into hell;   Acts 2:27;
1 Peter 3:19; Eph. 4:9
the third day he arose from the dead:
Luke 24:21-24
he ascended into heaven,   Eph. 4:8, 10
and sits at the right hand of Majesty—God the
Father Almighty;   Col. 3:1; Heb. 1:3

whence he shall return   Matt. 24:30
1 Thess. 4:14-17; Heb. 9:28
for those who are ready   Matt. 24:44-46;
2 Tim. 4:8
and watching, Mark 13:34-36; Titus 2:12, 13
to judge the quick and the dead. 2 Tim. 4:1;
Rev. 20:12

I believe Christ makes holy (sanctifies) ;
   1 Cor. 1:2; Heb. 10:10, 14
   and, in his righteousness, access is had to God.
   1 Cor. 1:30; Rom. 10:4

I believe in the Holy Spirit—   John 1:33
   promised by Jesus, sent by the Father—
   John 14:6, 7
   who manifests his indwelling by speaking
   John 3:8; John 15:26, 27
   in unknown languages, Isa. 28:11; Acts 10:46
   and gives gifts severally as he will.
   Heb. 2:4; 1 Cor. 12:4

I believe in the communion of the saints;
   1 Cor. 10:16, 17
   the forgiveness of sins (a God-made salvation) ;
   Eph. 4:32; Col. 2:13; 3:13
   man's responsibility; Phil. 2:12, 3:9; Heb. 2:3
   the resurrection of the body; John 5:28, 29;
   Acts 4:33
   and life everlasting.   Matt. 19:29
Amen.

           —James Moore Evans

The Church

BIBLE REFERENCES

"But now thus saith the Lord that created thee, O Jacob, and he that formed thee, O Israel, Fear not: for I have redeemed thee, I have called thee by thy name; thou art mine."   (Isa. 43:1)

"And the Lord their God shall save them in that day as the flock of his people: for they shall be as the stones of a crown, lifted up as an ensign upon his land."   (Zech. 9:16)

"Then they that feared the Lord spake often one to another: and the Lord hearkened, and heard it, and a book of remembrance was written before him for them that feared the Lord, and that thought upon his name. And they shall be mine, saith the Lord of hosts, in that day when I make up my jewels; and I will spare them, as a man spareth his own son that serveth him."   (Mal. 3:16, 17)

"And I say also unto thee, That thou art Peter, and upon this rock I will build my church; and the gates of hell shall not prevail against it.

(Matt. 16:18)

"But as many as received him, to them gave he power to become the sons of God, even to them that believe on his name."   (John 1:12)

"Now to him that is of power to stablish you according to my gospel, and the preaching of Jesus Christ, according to the revelation of the mystery, which was kept secret since the world began, but now is made manifest, and by the scriptures of the prophets, according to the commandment of the everlasting God, made known to all nations for the obedience of faith: to God only wise, be glory through Jesus Christ for ever. Amen."

(Rom. 16:25-27.)

"Now there are diversities of gifts, but the same Spirit. And there are differences of administrations, but the same Lord. And there are diversities of operations, but it is the same God which worketh all in all. But the manifestation of the Spirit is given to every man to profit withal. Now ye are the body of Christ, and members in particular. And God hath set some in the church, first apostles, secondarily prophets, thirdly teachers, after that miracles, then gifts of healings, helps, governments, diversities of tongues. Are all apostles? are all prophets? are all teachers? are all workers of miracles? have all the gifts of healing? do all speak with tongues? do all interpret? but covet earnestly the best gifts: and yet shew I unto you a more excellent way." (1 Cor. 12:4-7, 27-31)

"For I am jealous over you with godly jealousy: for I have espoused you to one husband, that I may present you as a chaste virgin to Christ."

(2 Cor. 11:2)

"Beside those things that are without, that which cometh upon me daily, the care of all the churches."

(2 Cor. 11:28)

"Now therefore ye are no more strangers and foreigners, but fellowcitizens with the saints and of the household of God; and are built upon the foundation of the apostles and prophets, Jesus Christ himself being the chief corner stone; in whom all the building fitly framed together groweth unto an holy temple in the Lord: in whom ye also are builded together for an habitation of God through the Spirit." (Eph. 2:19-22)

"Therefore as the church is subject unto Christ ... Christ also loved the church, and gave himself for it; that he might sanctify and cleanse it with the washing of water by the word, that he might present it to himself a glorious church, not having spot, or wrinkle, or any such thing; but that it should be holy and without blemish."

(Eph. 5:24-27)

"For we are members of his body, of his flesh, and of his bones." (Eph. 5: 30)

"If there be therefore any consolation in Christ, if any comfort of love, if any fellowship of the Spirit, if any bowels and mercies, fulfil ye my joy, that ye be likeminded, having the same love, being of one accord, of one mind. Let nothing be done through strife or vainglory; but in lowliness of mind let each esteem other better than themselves. Look not every man on his own things, but every man also on the things of others. Let this mind be in you, which was also in Christ Jesus." (Phil. 2:1-5)

"And he is the head of the body, the church:

37

who is the beginning, the firstborn from the dead; that in all things he might have the preeminence." (Col. 1:18)

"If any man teach otherwise, and consent not to wholesome words, even the words of our Lord Jesus Christ, and to the doctrine which is according to godliness; he is proud, knowing nothing, but doting about questions and strifes of words, whereof cometh envy, strife, railings, evil surmisings, perverse disputings of men of corrupt minds, and destitute of the truth, supposing that gain is godliness: from such withdraw thyself." (1 Tim. 6:3-5)

"But ye are come unto mount Sion, and unto the city of the living God, the heavenly Jerusalem, and to an innumerable company of angels, to the general assembly and church of the firstborn, which are written in heaven, and to God the Judge of all, and to the spirits of just men made perfect, and to Jesus the mediator of the new covenant, and to the blood of sprinkling, that speaketh better things than that of Abel." (Heb. 12:22-24)

A COVENANT

Having been led, as we believe by the Holy Spirit of God, to accept as our Saviour, the Lord Jesus Christ, in whose blood and righteousness alone we trust as the ground of our redemption; and having been buried with Him in baptism into the likeness of His death, and raised in the likeness of His resurrection, to walk in newness of life; and having thus been united to His visible church, we do now most joyfully and solemnly enter into covenant with God and with one another as one body in Christ.

We solemnly promise and engage that, by the aid of the Holy Spirit, we will love one another as brethren in the Lord; that we will exercise Christian care and watchfulness one for another, bearing one another's burdens and thus fulfill the law of Christ.

We engage to maintain secret and family devotion, to search the Scriptures with all diligence, and to train up our children in the nurture and admonition of the Lord.

We covenant that we will not forsake the assembling of ourselves together in the house of the Lord, but will regularly attend its services unless providentially hindered; that we will pray and labor for its prosperity through its doctrines, its ordinances, and its discipline; that we will earnestly and actively endeavor to win souls to our Saviour, realizing that apart from Him there is no hope and that He has left us in the world as His "ambassadors," in His Name to "seek and to save the lost."

We covenant that we will regularly and systematically give of our substance, as the Lord prospers us, for the support of an evangelical ministry amongst us, for the relief of the poor, and the spread of the gospel in the whole world; that we will endeavor to walk circumspectly in the world; to be just in our dealings, faithful in our engagements, and exemplary in our deportment; to remember each other in prayer, to comfort each other in sickness and distress; to cultivate Christian sympathy and courtesy; to be slow to take offense, ready for reconciliation, and mindful of the teaching of our Saviour to secure it without delay.

Desiring the triumph of Christ above all earthly good, and joyfully hoping for His coming again in heavenly glory, we covenant that, by the help of His enabling Spirit, we will seek first the kingdom of God and His righteousness, trusting Him to add unto us all temporal necessities and the fullness of heavenly grace.

Worship

CALLS TO WORSHIP

"Give unto the Lord the glory due unto his name: bring an offering and come before him: worship the Lord in the beauty of holiness." (1 Chron. 16:29)

"Be wise now therefore, O ye kings: be instructed, ye judges of the earth. Serve the Lord with fear, and rejoice with trembling. Kiss the Son, lest he be angry, and ye perish from the way, when his wrath is kindled but a little. Blessed are all they that put their trust in him." (Ps. 2:10-12)

"I will praise thee, O Lord, with my whole heart; I will shew forth all thy marvellous works. I will be glad and rejoice in thee: I will sing praises to thy name, O thou most High." (Ps. 9:1, 2)

"Sing praises to the Lord, which dwelleth in Zion: declare among the people his doings." (Ps. 9:11)

"Give unto the Lord, O ye mighty, give unto the Lord glory and strength. Give unto the Lord the glory due unto his name; worship the Lord in the beauty of holiness." (Ps. 29:1, 2)

"O love the Lord, all ye his saints: for the Lord preserveth the faithful, and plentifully rewardeth the proud doer. Be of good courage, and he shall strengthen your heart, all ye that hope in the Lord." (Ps. 31:23, 24)

"Rejoice in the Lord, O ye righteous: for praise is comely for the upright. Praise the Lord with harp: sing unto him with the psaltery and an instrument of ten strings. Sing unto him a new song; play skillfully with a loud noise. For the word of the Lord is right; and all his works are done in truth. He loveth righteousness and judgment: the earth is full of the goodness of the Lord." (Ps. 33:1-5)

"Our soul waiteth for the Lord: he is our help and our shield. For our heart shall rejoice in him, because we have trusted in his holy name. Let thy mercy, O Lord, be upon us, according as we hope in thee." (Ps. 33:20-22)

"O magnify the Lord with me, and let us exalt his name together." (Ps. 34:3)

"The Lord is nigh unto them that are of a broken heart; and saveth such as be of a contrite spirit." (Ps. 34:18)

"As the hart panteth after the water brooks, so panteth my soul after thee, O God." (Ps. 42:1)

"O send out thy light and thy truth: let them lead me; let them bring me unto thy holy hill, and to thy tabernacles. Then will I go unto the altar of God, unto God my exceeding joy: yea, upon the harp will I praise thee, O God my God." (Ps. 43:3, 4)

"Be still, and know that I am God: I will be exalted among the heathen, I will be exalted in the earth. The Lord of hosts is with us; the God of Jacob is our refuge. Selah." (Ps. 46:10, 11)

"Make a joyful noise unto God, all ye lands: sing forth the honour of his name: make his praise glorious. Say unto God, How terrible art thou in thy works! through the greatness of thy power shall thine enemies submit themselves unto thee. All the earth shall worship thee, and shall sing unto thee; they shall sing to thy name. Selah." (Ps. 66:1-4)

"O bless our God, ye people, and make the voice of his praise to be heard: which holdeth our soul in life, and suffereth not our feet to be moved." (Ps. 66:8, 9)

"Let the people praise thee, O God; let all the people praise thee." (Ps. 67:3)

"Unto thee, O God, do we give thanks, unto thee do we give thanks: for that thy name is near thy wondrous works declare." (Ps. 75:1)

"Behold, O God our shield, and look upon the face of thine anointed. For a day in thy courts is better than a thousand. I had rather be a doorkeeper in the house of my God, than to dwell in the tents of wickedness." (Ps. 84:9, 10)

"All nations whom thou hast made shall come and worship before thee, O Lord; and shall glorify thy name. For thou art great, and doest wondrous things: thou art God alone." (Ps. 86:9, 10)

"It is a good thing to give thanks unto the Lord, and to sing praises unto thy name, O most High: to show forth thy lovingkindness in the morning, and thy faithfulness every night, upon an instrument of ten strings, and upon the psaltery; upon the harp with a solemn sound." (Ps. 92:1-3)

"O come, let us sing unto the Lord: let us make a joyful noise to the rock of our salvation. Let us come before his presence with thanksgiving, and make a joyful noise unto him with psalms."

(Ps. 95:1, 2)

"O come, let us worship and bow down: let us kneel before the Lord our maker. For he is our God; and we are the people of his pasture, and the sheep of his hand." (Ps. 95:6, 7)

"O sing unto the Lord a new song: sing unto the Lord, all the earth. Sing unto the Lord, bless his name; shew forth his salvation from day to day."

(Ps. 96:1, 2)

"Give unto the Lord the glory due unto his name: bring an offering, and come into his courts. O worship the Lord in the beauty of holiness: fear before him, all the earth." (Ps. 96:8, 9)

"Exalt ye the Lord our God, and worship at his footstool; for he is holy." (Ps. 99:5)

"Make a joyful noise unto the Lord, all ye lands. Serve the Lord with gladness: come before his presence with singing." (Ps. 100:1, 2)

"Let them exalt him also in the congregation of the people, and praise him in the assembly of the elders." (Ps. 107:32)

"This is the day which the Lord hath made; we will rejoice and be glad in it." (Ps. 118:24)

"I was glad when they said unto me, Let us go into the house of the Lord." (Ps. 122:1)

"But they that wait upon the Lord shall renew their strength; they shall mount up with wings as eagles; they shall run, and not be weary; and they shall walk, and not faint." (Isa. 40:31)

"Seek ye the Lord while he may be found, call ye upon him while he is near: let the wicked forsake his way, and the unrighteous man his thoughts: and let him return unto the Lord, and he will have mercy upon him; and to our God, for he will abundantly pardon." (Isa. 55:6, 7)

"But the Lord is in his holy temple: let all the earth keep silence before him." (Hab. 2:20)

"Let us draw near with a true heart in full assurance of faith, having our hearts sprinkled from an evil conscience, and our bodies washed with pure water." (Heb. 10:22)

"Fear God, and give glory to him; for the hour of his judgment is come: and worship him that made heaven, and earth, and the sea, and the fountains of waters." (Rev. 14:7)

"Who shall not fear thee, O Lord, and glorify thy name? for thou only art holy: for all nations shall come and worship before thee; for thy judgments are made manifest." (Rev. 15:4)

OFFERTORY REFERENCES

"Speak unto the children of Israel, that they bring me an offering: of every man that giveth it willingly with his heart ye shall take my offering."   (Ex. 25:2)

"Take ye from among you an offering unto the Lord: whosoever is of a willing heart, let him bring it, an offering of the Lord; gold, and silver, and brass, and blue, and purple, and scarlet, and fine linen, and goats' hair, and rams' skins dyed red, and badgers' skins, and shittim wood, and oil for the light, and spices for anointing oil, and for the sweet incense, and onyx stones, and stones to be set for the ephod, and for the breastplate."

(Ex. 35:5-9)

"If ye walk in my statutes, and keep my commandments, and do them; then I will give you rain in due season, and the land shall yield her increase, and the trees of the field shall yield their fruit."   (Lev. 26:3, 4)

"And all the tithe of the land, whether of the seed of the land, or of the fruit of the tree, is the Lord's: it is holy unto the Lord."   (Lev. 27:30)

"But thou shalt remember the Lord thy God: for it is he that giveth thee power to get wealth, that he may establish his covenant which he sware unto thy fathers, as it is this day."   (Deut. 8:18)

"Then the people rejoiced, for that they offered willingly, because with perfect heart they offered willingly to the Lord: and David the king also rejoiced with great joy." (1 Chron. 29:9)

"Also that day they offered great sacrifices, and rejoiced: for God had made them rejoice with great joy: the wives also and the children rejoiced: so that the joy of Jerusalem was heard even afar off." (Neh. 12:43)

"Blessed is he that considereth the poor: the Lord will deliver him in time of trouble." (Ps. 41:1)

"Be not thou afraid when one is made rich, when the glory of his house is increased; for when he dieth he shall carry nothing away: his glory shall not descend after him." (Ps. 49:16, 17)

"For every beast of the forest is mine, and the cattle upon a thousand hills. I know all the fowls of the mountains: and the wild beasts of the field are mine. If I were hungry, I would not tell thee: for the world is mine, and the fulness thereof. Will I eat the flesh of bulls, or drink the blood of goats? Offer unto God thanksgiving; and pay thy vows unto the most High: and call upon me in the day of trouble: I will deliver thee, and thou shalt glorify me." (Ps. 50:10-15)

"Honour the Lord with thy substance, and with the firstfruits of all thine increase." (Prov. 3:9)

"Give a portion to seven, and also to eight; for thou knowest not what evil shall be upon the earth." (Eccl. 11:2)

"Bring ye all the tithes into the storehouse, that

there may be meat in mine house, and prove me now herewith, saith the Lord of hosts, if I will not open you the windows of heaven, and pour you out a blessing, that there shall not be room enough to receive it." (Mal. 3:10)

"Lay not up for yourselves treasures upon earth, where moth and rust doth corrupt, and where thieves break through and steal: but lay up for yourselves treasures in heaven, where neither moth nor rust doth corrupt, and where thieves do not break through nor steal: for where your treasure is, there will your heart be also." (Matt. 6:19-21)

"Therefore all things whatsoever ye would that men should do to you, do ye even so to them: for this is the law and the prophets." (Matt. 7:12)

"Heal the sick, cleanse the lepers, raise the dead, cast out devils: freely ye have received, freely give." (Matt. 10:8)

"Then saith he unto them, Render therefore unto Caesar the things which are Caesar's; and unto God the things that are God's." (Matt. 22:21)

"Give, and it shall be given unto you; good measure, pressed down, and shaken together, and running over, shall men give into your bosom. For with the same measure that ye mete withal it shall be measured to you again." (Luke 6:38)

"And with great power gave the apostles witness of the resurrection of the Lord Jesus: and great grace was upon them all. Neither was there any

among them that lacked: for as many as were pos-
sessors of lands or houses sold them, and brought
the prices of the things that were sold, and laid them
down at the apostles' feet: and distribution was made
unto every man according as he had need."

(Acts 4:33-35)

"Then the disciples, every man according to his
ability, determined to send relief unto the brethren
which dwelt in Judaea." (Acts 11:29)

"I have shewed you all things, how that so labour-
ing ye ought to support the weak, and to remember
the words of the Lord Jesus, how he said, It is more
blessed to give than to receive." (Acts 20:35)

"Not slothful in business; fervent in spirit; serving
the Lord." (Rom. 12:11)

"Therefore, my beloved brethren, be ye stedfast,
unmoveable, always abounding in the work of the
Lord, forasmuch as ye know that your labour is not
in vain in the Lord." (1 Cor. 15:58)

"Upon the first day of the week let every one
of you lay by him in store, as God hath prospered
him, that there be no gatherings when I come."

(1 Cor. 16:2)

"For if there be first a willing mind, it is accepted
according to that a man hath, and not according
to that he hath not." (2 Cor. 8:12)

"Every man according as he purposeth in his heart,
so let him give; not grudgingly, or of necessity: for
God loveth a cheerful giver. And God is able to make

all grace abound toward you; that ye, always having all sufficiency in all things, may abound to every good work." (2 Cor. 9:7, 8)

"Charge them that are rich in this world, that they be not highminded, nor trust in uncertain riches, but in the living God, who giveth us richly all things to enjoy; that they do good, that they be rich in good works, ready to distribute, willing to communicate; laying up in store for themselves a good foundation against the time to come, that they may lay hold on eternal life." (1 Tim. 6:17-19)

"For God is not unrighteous to forget your work and labour of love, which ye have shewed toward his name, in that ye have ministered to the saints, and do minister." (Heb. 6:10)

"If a brother or sister be naked, and destitute of daily food, and one of you say unto them, Depart in peace, be ye warmed and filled; notwithstanding ye give them not those things which are needful to the body; what doth it profit?" (James 2:15, 16)

"As every man hath received the gift, even so minister the same one to another, as good stewards of the manifold grace of God." (1 Peter 4:10)

"But whoso hath this world's good, and seeth his brother have need, and shutteth up his bowels of compassion from him, how dwelleth the love of God in him?" (1 John 3:17)

DOXOLOGIES

"Give ear to my words, O Lord, consider my meditation. Hearken unto the voice of my cry, my King, and my God: for unto thee will I pray. My voice shalt thou hear in the morning, O Lord; in the morning will I direct my prayer unto thee, and will look up." (Ps. 5:1-3)

"O give thanks unto the Lord; call upon his name: make known his deeds among the people. Sing unto him, sing psalms unto him: talk ye of all his wondrous works. Glory ye in his holy name: let the heart of them rejoice that seek the Lord." (Ps. 105:1-3)

"Praise ye the Lord. O give thanks unto the Lord; for he is good: for his mercy endureth for ever. Who can utter the mighty acts of the Lord? who can shew forth all his praise?" (Ps. 106:1, 2)

"O give thanks unto the Lord, for he is good: for his mercy endureth for ever." (Ps. 107:1)

"Now to him that is of power to stablish you according to my gospel, and the preaching of Jesus Christ, according to the revelation of the mystery, which was kept secret since the world began, but now is made manifest, and by the scriptures of the prophets, according to the commandment of the everlasting God, made known to all nations for the obedience of faith: to God only wise, be glory through Jesus Christ for ever. Amen."

(Rom. 16:25-27)

"Now unto him that is able to do exceeding abundantly above all that we ask or think, according to the power that worketh in us, unto him be glory in the church by Christ Jesus throughout all ages, world without end. Amen."   (Eph. 3:20, 21)

"Giving thanks always for all things unto God and the Father in the name of our Lord Jesus Christ."
(Eph. 5:20)

"Now unto him that is able to keep you from falling, and to present you faultless before the presence of his glory with exceeding joy, to the only wise God our Saviour, be glory and majesty, dominion and power, both now and ever. Amen."

(Jude 24, 25)

"And from Jesus Christ, who is the faithful witness, and the first begotten of the dead, and the prince of the kings of the earth. Unto him that loved us, and washed us from our sins in his own blood, and hath made us kings and priests unto God and his Father; to him be glory and dominion for ever and ever. Amen."   (Rev. 1:5, 6)

BENEDICTIONS

"The Lord bless thee, and keep thee: the Lord make his face shine upon thee, and be gracious unto thee: the Lord lift up his countenance upon thee, and give thee peace." (Num. 6:24-26)

"And now, brethren, I commend you to God, and to the word of his grace, which is able to build you up, and to give you an inheritance among all them which are sanctified." (Acts 20:32)

"Now the God of patience and consolation grant you to be likeminded one toward another according to Christ Jesus: that ye may with one mind and one mouth glorify God, even the Father of our Lord Jesus Christ." (Rom. 15:5, 6)

"Now the God of hope fill you with all joy and peace in believing, that ye may abound in hope, through the power of the Holy Ghost." (Rom. 15:13)

"Grace be unto you, and peace, from God our Father, and from the Lord Jesus Christ." (1 Cor. 1:3)

"Be perfect, be of good comfort, be of one mind, live in peace; and the God of love and peace shall be with you. . . . The grace of the Lord Jesus Christ, and the love of God, and the communion of the Holy Ghost, be with you all. Amen."

(2 Cor. 13:11, 14)

"Now unto him that is able to do exceeding abundantly above all that we ask or think, according to the power that worketh in us, unto him be glory in the church by Christ Jesus throughout all ages, world without end. Amen." (Eph. 3:20, 21)

"Grace be with all them that love our Lord Jesus Christ in sincerity. Amen." (Eph. 6:24)

"And the peace of God, which passeth all understanding . . . keep your hearts and minds through Christ Jesus." (Phil. 4:7)

"Now unto God and our Father be glory for ever and ever. Amen." (Phil. 4:20)

"The grace of our Lord Jesus Christ be with you all. Amen." (Phil. 4:23)

"And the very God of peace sanctify you wholly; and I pray God your whole spirit and soul and body be preserved blameless unto the coming of our Lord Jesus Christ." (1 Thess. 5:23)

"Now our Lord Jesus Christ himself, and God, even our Father, which hath loved us, and hath given us everlasting consolation and good hope through grace, comfort your hearts, and stablish you in every good word and work." (2 Thess. 2:16, 17)

"Unto————in the faith: Grace, mercy, and peace, from God our Father and Jesus Christ our Lord." (1 Tim. 1:2)

"The grace of our Lord Jesus Christ be with your spirit. Amen." (Philemon 25)

"Now the God of peace, that brought again from the dead our Lord Jesus, that great shepherd of the sheep, through the blood of the everlasting covenant, make you perfect in every good work to do his will, working in you that which is wellpleasing in his sight, through Jesus Christ; to whom be glory for ever and ever. Amen." (Heb. 13:20, 21)

"But the God of all grace, who hath called us unto his eternal glory by Christ Jesus, after that ye have suffered a while, make you perfect, stablish, strengthen, settle you. To him be glory and dominion for ever and ever. Amen." (1 Peter 5:10, 11)

"Now unto him that is able to keep you from falling, and to present you faultless before the presence of his glory with exceeding joy, to the only wise God our Saviour, be glory and majesty, dominion and power, both now and ever. Amen."

(Jude 24, 25)

"The grace of our Lord Jesus Christ be with you all. Amen." (Rev. 22:21)

Dedication of Children

BIBLE REFERENCES

"And Joseph said unto his father, They are my sons, whom God hath given me in this place. And he said, Bring them, I pray thee, unto me, and I will bless them."   (Gen. 48:9)

"So Hannah rose up after they had eaten in Shiloh, ... And she vowed a vow, and said, O Lord of hosts, if thou wilt indeed look on the affliction of thine handmaid, and remember me, and not forget thine handmaid, but wilt give unto thine handmaid a man child, then I will give him unto the Lord all the days of his life, and there shall no razor come upon his head.... Then Eli answered and said, Go in peace: and the God of Israel grant thee thy petition that thou hast asked of him.... And they rose up in the morning early, and worshipped before the Lord, and returned, and came to their house to Ramah: and Elkanah knew Hannah his wife; and the Lord remembered her. Wherefore it came to pass, when the time was come about after Hannah had conceived, that she bare a son, and called his name Samuel, saying, Because I have asked him of the Lord.... And when she had weaned him, she took him up with her, with three bullocks, and one ephah of flour, and a bottle of wine, and brought him unto the house of the Lord in Shiloh: and the child was young. And they slew a bullock, and brought the child to Eli. And she said, Oh my lord, as thy soul liveth, my lord, I am the woman that stood by thee here, praying unto the Lord. For this child I prayed; and the Lord hath given me my petition which I asked of him: therefore also I have lent him to the Lord; as long as he liveth he shall be lent to the Lord. And he worshipped the Lord there." (1 Sam. 1:9, 11, 17, 19, 20, 24-28)

"And all Judah stood before the Lord, with their little ones, their wives, and their children."

(2 Chron. 20:13)

"Lo, children are an heritage of the Lord: and the fruit of the womb is his reward." (Ps. 127:3)

"Train up a child in the way he should go: and when he is old, he will not depart from it."
(Prov. 22:6)

"And they brought unto him also infants, that he would touch them: but when his disciples saw it, they rebuked them. But Jesus called them unto him, and said, Suffer little children to come unto me, and forbid them not: for of such is the kingdom of God. Verily I say unto you, Whosoever shall not receive the kingdom of God as a little child shall in no wise enter therein." (Luke 18:15-17)

A DEDICATION SERVICE

INTRODUCTION

The pastor may introduce the dedication in words similar to the following:

Today we have————(number) babies to be dedicated to the Lord. How thankful we are for this God-given increase in our church. Will the parents bring the children to be dedicated.

BIBLICAL AUTHORITY

Suitable music should be played while the parents take their places with their children.

Then the pastor may read the following, or another suitable passage of Scripture:

"And they brought young children unto him (Jesus), that he should touch them: and his disciples rebuked those that brought them. But when Jesus saw it, he was much displeased, and said unto them, Suffer the little children to come unto me, and forbid them not: for of such is the kingdom of God. Verily I say unto you, Whosoever shall not receive the kingdom of God as a little child, he shall not enter therein. And he took them up in his arms, put his hands upon them, and blessed them."

(Mark 10:13-16)

PRAYER

This prayer is a prayer of thanksgiving for God's gift of children, and for Christ's love for them and for the children who are to be dedicated.

ADDRESS TO THE CONGREGATION

The pastor may speak extemporaneously to the audience concerning the significance of dedication; or he may say:

The dedication of children unto the Lord had its beginning in early Old Testament days. Hannah is an example. She came to the temple to pray for a son. And she promised God that if He would give her a man child she would "give him unto the Lord all the days of his life." God gave her a son. She called his name Samuel. And she cared for him until he was old enough to return to full-time work in the temple. Then she gave him to the ministry to which he had been called by God. In this dedication Hannah was joined by her husband, Elkanah. What they did was in recognition that their son was a gift from God. And their act of dedication was a returning back to God of that which belonged to Him.

This dedication serves as an example, but it is more than just an example. It is a pattern for all dedications of little children from that day to this.

ADDRESS TO THE PARENTS

The pastor may continue to speak extemporaneously, addressing the parents. Or he may say:

————— (names of parents), in presenting this child (your children) for dedication you not only signify your faith in Christ and the Christian way of life, but you also indicate your desire that he (she) should grow to know the Lord and live a Christian life.

You come with thanks in your hearts for the little life which God has placed in your care.

But, in order for this dedication to be complete, it is necessary for you, not only to thank God but to say to Him, "We give back to Thee, Lord, that which is really Thine own. Make of him (her) what Thou wilt. Use him (her) to Thine eternal glory. Keep him (her) in Thy will until the day that Thou shalt take him (her) to be with Thyself."

You can do nothing better than to put the child in God's hands, for only God knows what possibilities there are wrapped up in this little life. And only God can develop in this life all the possibilities that are there.

And you have still another responsibility in addition to that of surrendering the child to God. Just as Moses was given back to his mother, Jochebed, to rear as a son of Pharaoh's daughter, so will this child be given back to you to rear for God. You will need to listen in prayer to know what God's instructions to you will be. You will need to pass on to the child the things which God tells you to teach him (her). You will need to be willing to do God's will when it crosses your own. And you will need to be willing to surrender the child to whatever ministry God may choose for him (her) in years to come.

If you are willing, join me now in prayer of dedication.

PRAYER OF DEDICATION

The minister may speak for the parents in giving the baby to God in prayer, and ask God's blessing on each of the parents.

ACT OF DEDICATION

The minister may take each child in his arms, give thanks and dedicate it, using words somewhat as follows:

We thank Thee, Lord, for little———— (name), and for what Thou wilt do with this life. And now I dedicate you,———— (name), in the name of the Father, and of the Son, and of the Holy Ghost.

GIVING OF CERTIFICATES[1]

After all of the children have been dedicated music should be played softly while the minister gives certificates of dedication, saying:

Here is a certificate of dedication of the lovely child which the Lord has given you.

Appropriate music should continue while the parents take their seats in the audience.

—*Ray Wilkerson*

---

[1] It is optional for the minister to give certificates at the time of dedication or at a later time.

A DEDICATION SERVICE

INTRODUCTION

The minister shall call the parents who have brought children for dedication to present themselves with their children before the altar.

Then the minister may say:

BIBLICAL AUTHORITY

When the Lord Jesus dwelt as the Son of Man among men, the Scriptures say that "they brought young children to Him, that He should touch them: and his disciples rebuked those that brought them. But when Jesus saw it, he was much displeased, and said unto them, Suffer the little children to come unto me, and forbid them not: for of such is the kingdom of God. And he took them up in his arms, put his hands upon them, and blessed them."

(Mark 10:13, 14, 16)

ADDRESS TO THE CONGREGATION

In our day little children are brought to ministers who, as representatives of the Lord, receive them, pray for the protecting hand of the Lord to be upon them, and bless them in an act of dedication. The dedication is unto the Lord, to the end that He may keep them and bless them all the days of their lives.

Parents who bring their children for dedication, by the very act, signify their faith in the Christian way of life. They also indicate their desire that their children should grow up to know the Lord, to live according to His will, and to live eternally in the blessedness which God has decreed for those who love Him.

The act of dedication does not automatically make the children Christian. Instead, it is a point of beginning in which parents, having committed the children to God for His care in matters beyond human wisdom and understanding, enter into partnership with the church to teach them early to fear the Lord; to direct their minds to the Holy Scriptures, their feet to the sanctuary, and their hearts to Christ as their Saviour; to bring them up in the nurture and admonition of the Lord.

PLEDGE

The minister shall then address the parents before him, calling them by name if there is only one family, but substituting some other designation such as "you who have brought children for dedication," if there are too many families to be named.

Will you,————— (parents), endeavor to do so by the help of God? If so, answer, "I will."

The parents reply:

I will.

DEDICATION AND CHARGE

Then the minister, taking the child (or each child in succession) in his arms, shall say:

As God's minister, I take————— (child's name) from you. Now let us give him (her) to the Lord.

The minister, continuing to hold the child, offers a dedicatory prayer.

After prayer, the child is returned to the parents with the following admonition:

Now we lend————— (child's name) back to you to rear in the fear and admonition of the Lord.

—William E. Pickthorn

A DEDICATION SERVICE

Introduction

Let some children's song be sung while the parents bring the child to the altar where the minister shall meet them.

Biblical Authority

Appropriate Scriptures may be read as the minister stands before the altar:

"Then were there brought unto him little children, that he should put his hands on them, and pray: and the disciples rebuked them. But Jesus said, Suffer little children, and forbid them not, to come unto me: for of such is the kingdom of heaven. And he laid his hands on them, and departed thence."

(Matt. 19:13-15)

Address to the Congregation

To the congregation or assembled friends the minister may say:

The family is a divine institution ordained of God from the beginning of time. Children are a heritage of the Lord committed by Him to their parents for care, protection, and training for His glory. It is meet that all parents recognize this obligation and their responsibility to God in this matter. Jochebed of old trained her own child, Moses, after having given him to the Lord. Hannah recognized that her child was Jehovah's. The Virgin

Mary also brought the infant Jesus to the temple. The parents of this child likewise recognize the sacredness of their charge and now bring back to the Lord the treasure with which the Lord has entrusted them. In so doing they recognize and hereby publicly acknowledge their responsibility for the nurture and admonition of this child in the ways of righteousness and godliness.

Charge to the Parents

The minister shall then address the parents as follows:

In the sight of God and in the presence of these witnesses do you solemnly undertake to bring up this child in the fear and admonition of the Lord?

The parents shall answer:

We do.

The minister shall continue:

Do you promise early to seek to lead him (her) to accept Jesus Christ as Saviour and Lord?

The parents shall answer:

We do.

The minister shall then end the charge, saying:

Do you promise as far as in you lies to set before him (her) examples of godly and consistent lives?

The parents shall answer:

We do.

Dedication

Then, taking the child in his arms or laying hands upon its head, the minister shall say:

In the name of the Lord Jesus I dedicate this child,
———— (name) , to God and His holy service.

PRAYER

The minister shall then offer a dedicatory prayer. The congregation may sing another hymn in conclusion.

—*Martin H. Heicksen*

A DEDICATION SERVICE

INTRODUCTION

At an appropriate time in the service a hymn shall be sung and the parents, with their children, invited to stand in the front of the church.

BIBLICAL AUTHORITY

The minister, or a person appointed by him, may read from the Scriptures:

"But Hannah went not up; for she said unto her husband, I will not go up until the child be weaned, and then I will bring him, that he may appear before the Lord, and there abide for ever. And she said, Oh my lord, as thy soul liveth, my lord, I am the woman that stood by thee here, praying unto the Lord. Therefore also I have lent him to the Lord; as long as he liveth he shall be lent to the Lord. And he worshipped the Lord there."

(1 Sam. 1:22, 26, 28)

"Then were there brought unto him little children, that he should put his hands on them, and pray: and the disciples rebuked them. But Jesus said, Suffer little children, and forbid them not, to come unto me: for of such is the kingdom of heaven. And he laid his hands on them, and departed thence."

(Matt. 19:13-15)

"And when the days of her purification according to the law of Moses were accomplished, they brought him to Jerusalem, to present him to the Lord."

(Luke 2:22)

71

ADDRESS

The presenting of a child in dedication or christening is a serious matter. It involves responsibilities with which we shall be charged, and a responsibility which God has promised to take upon Himself toward each life which is put in His care.

CHARGE TO THE PARENTS

Parents, the first responsibility is yours. Before God, to whom you bring your child for christening, I charge each of you:

That you live an exemplary life before the child that he (she) may by example know what it is to be a Christian;

That you make your home a "school" where he (she) shall receive Christian instruction;

That you shall see that he (she) is taken to the church for additional instruction;

That you shall pray for his (her) salvation when he (she) reaches the age of accountability, and that you shall endeavor to lead him (her) to Christ.

If you are willing to accept this charge, answer, "I will."

The parents shall each say:
I will.

CHARGE TO THE CONGREGATION

The minister shall then address the congregation. He may ask the congregation to stand to receive its charge, and then say:

The church which, through its minister, accepts

a child in dedication assumes a responsibility before God. And in view of this responsibility, I charge you who are members:

That you will do all that you can to provide and support a place of worship and instruction in this community where this child, should he (she) continue to live here, may hear the full counsel of God's Word;

That you will all covenant together to set an example by your lives and to maintain an atmosphere in your church which shall inspire him (her) to desire the Christian way of life;

That, as God shall remind you, you shall pray for his (her) salvation.

Those of you who are willing to accept this charge, please answer, "With God's help, we will."

The congregation, led by an officer who has been instructed in advance to lead in the response, shall say:

With God's help, we will.

God's Promise

If the congregation is standing it should be seated at this point. Then the minister may say:

On the authority of God's holy Word, and as a minister of Christ's church, I affirm that—if we faithfully keep our pledges to God—God will:

Through the Holy Spirit convict him (her) (each of these children) of sin as he (she) comes to age of accountability;

Make the love of Christ, His Son, known to him (her);

Bless and guide His child throughout all his (her) Christian life.

ANOINTING

The minister may then take the child, or each of the children in succession, in his arms and say:
————— (name), I anoint you with oil as a symbol of the Holy Spirit under whose protection and guidance we are sealing you; and I dedicate you unto God, in the name of the Father, and of the Son, and of the Holy Spirit.

PRAYER

The minister shall ask the congregation to stand as witnesses as he prays for God's blessing of health, salvation, and a good life for the child, or children.

If only one child has been presented for dedication the minister shall continue to hold the child in his arms as he prays. Then, handing the child back to the parents, he shall pray for the parents.

If two or more children have been presented for dedication the parents shall continue to hold the children as the minister prays for the children, and then for all of the parents.

Finally, the minister shall pray for the congregation.

—*J. Calvin Holsinger*

A DEDICATION SERVICE

BIBLICAL AUTHORITY

"They brought young children to him, that he should touch them. . . . And he took them up in his arms, put his hands upon them, and blessed them."
(Mark 10:13, 16)

THE AGREEMENT OF DEDICATION

GOD'S PART: "The mercy of the Lord is from everlasting to everlasting upon them that fear him, and his righteousness unto children's children; to such as keep his covenant, and to those that remember his commandments to do them." (Ps. 103:17, 18)

"It is not the will of your Father which is in heaven, that one of these little ones should perish."
(Matt. 18:14)

THE PARENTS' PART: "And these words, which I command thee this day, shall be in thine heart: and thou shalt teach them diligently unto thy children, and shalt talk of them when thou sittest in thine house, and when thou walkest by the way, and when thou liest down, and when thou risest up."

(Deut. 6:6, 7)

THE CHARGE TO THE PARENTS

The minister shall charge the parents, using words similar to the following:

In this service of dedication we declare our faith in God; we recognize these children as His gifts to our homes; we promise to nurture them in the knowledge of God and in the spirit of Jesus Christ—dedicating them, as far as we may, to the service of God and of their fellows, trusting that they may ratify this dedication when they reach the years of discretion.

Do you so promise?

Each of the parents shall answer:

I do.

THE ACT OF DEDICATION

The minister may now conclude in words similar to the following:

I now dedicate these children to the Christian life, to the worship of God, and to the service of their fellowmen; in the name of the Father, and of the Son, and of the Holy Ghost. Amen.

PRAYER OF DEDICATION

There shall be an extemporaneous prayer of dedication by the minister, or someone appointed by him.

BENEDICTION

A suitable hymn may be sung and, if the service is to be concluded at this point, the benediction may be pronounced while the parents and the children still stand before the minister.

—Allan A. Swift

Water Baptism

BIBLE REFERENCES

"Then cometh Jesus from Galilee to Jordan unto John, to be baptized of him. But John forbad him, saying, I have need to be baptized of thee, and comest thou to me? And Jesus answering said unto him, Suffer it to be so now: for thus it becometh us to fulfil all righteousness. Then he suffered him. And Jesus, when he was baptized, went up straightway out of the water: and, lo, the heavens were opened unto him, and he saw the Spirit of God descending like a dove, and lighting upon him: and lo a voice from heaven, saying, This is my beloved Son, in whom I am well pleased." (Matt. 3:13-17)

"The baptism of John, whence was it? from heaven, or of men? And they reasoned with themselves, saying, If we shall say, From heaven; he will say unto us, Why did ye not then believe him? But if we shall say, Of men; we fear the people; for all hold John as a prophet. And they answered Jesus, and said, We cannot tell." (Matt. 21:25-27)

"And Jesus came and spake unto them, saying, All power is given unto me in heaven and in earth. Go ye therefore, and teach all nations, baptizing them in the name of the Father, and of the Son, and of the Holy Ghost: teaching them to observe all things whatsoever I have commanded you: and, lo, I am with you alway, even unto the end of the world. Amen." (Matt. 28:18-20)

"And he said unto them, Go ye into all the world, and preach the gospel to every creature. He that believeth and is baptized shall be saved; but he that believeth not shall be damned."

(Mark 16:15, 16)

"And they asked him, and said unto him, Why baptizest thou then, if thou be not that Christ, nor Elias, neither that prophet?" (John 1:25)

"And I knew him not: but that he should be made manifest to Israel, therefore am I come baptizing with water." (John 1:31)

"After these things came Jesus and his disciples into the land of Judaea; and there he tarried with them, and baptized. And John also was baptizing in Aenon near to Salim, because there was much water there: and they came, and were baptized."

(John 3:22, 23)

"Though Jesus himself baptized not, but his disciples." (John 4:2)

"Then Peter said unto them, Repent, and be baptized every one of you in the name of Jesus Christ for the remission of sins, and ye shall receive the gift of the Holy Ghost." (Acts 2:38)

"And he commanded the chariot to stand still: and they went down both into the water, both Philip and the eunuch; and he baptized him."

(Acts 8:38)

"And he took them the same hour of the night, and washed their stripes; and was baptized he and all his, straightway. And when he had brought them into his house, he set meat before them, and rejoiced, believing in God with all his house."

(Acts 16:33, 34)

"And Crispus, the chief ruler of the synagogue, believed on the Lord with all his house; and many of the Corinthians hearing believed, and were baptized." (Acts 18:8)

"And now why tarriest thou? arise, and be baptized, and wash away thy sins, calling on the name of the Lord." (Acts 22:16)

"Know ye not, that so many of us as were baptized into Jesus Christ were baptized into his death? Therefore we are buried with him by baptism into death: that like as Christ was raised up from the dead by the glory of the Father, even so we also should walk in newness of life. For if we have been planted together in the likeness of his death, we shall be also in the likeness of his resurrection." (Rom. 6:3-5)

"And were all baptized unto Moses in the cloud and in the sea." (1 Cor. 10:2)

"For as many of you as have been baptized into Christ have put on Christ." (Gal. 3:27)

"And ye are complete in him, which is the head of all principality and power: ... buried with him in baptism, wherein also ye are risen with him through the faith of the operation of God, who hath raised him from the dead." (Col. 2:10, 12)

A BAPTISMAL SERVICE

The baptismal service may be held in a baptistry, an outdoor pool, or in running water. The minister should be certain that the candidates understand thoroughly the ceremony through which they will pass and that they have experienced a change of heart. The candidates should understand that baptism is a declaration of dedication and a symbol of one's faith.

INVOCATION

The prayer should be for God's blessing upon the service and on the candidates who are to be baptized.

BIBLICAL AUTHORITY

"And Jesus came and spake unto them, saying, All power is given unto me in heaven and in earth. Go ye therefore, and teach all nations, baptizing them in the name of the Father, and of the Son, and of the Holy Ghost: teaching them to observe all things whatsoever I have commanded you: and, lo, I am with you alway, even unto the end of the world."

(Matt. 28:18-20)

"Then Peter said unto them, Repent, and be baptized every one of you in the name of Jesus Christ for the remission of sins, and ye shall receive the gift of the Holy Ghost. For the promise is unto you, and to your children, and to all that are afar off, even as many as the Lord our God shall call."

(Acts 2:38, 39)

Address to the Congregation

At this point it is appropriate to speak on the meaning of baptism in water. A suitable text may be selected from the Biblical references at the beginning of this section.

Address to the Candidates

The candidates may be asked to apply to themselves the meaning of baptism: dedicating themselves, and pledging themselves to a life of continued consecration to the teachings of Christ.

The Act of Baptism

The pastor shall enter the water, followed by the candidates—singly if the space is small, or in a group if the space is sufficiently large.

Each candidate shall stand in turn beside the pastor, and facing the congregation, as the pastor asks:

Do you acknowledge and profess the Christian faith as taught in the Holy Scriptures? If so, answer, "I do."

The candidate shall say:

I do.

Do you believe in Jesus Christ, the only begotten Son of God, and the only Saviour from sin? If so, answer, "I do."

The candidate shall again say:

I do.

Are you determined by the grace of God to commit

yourself daily to Christ as the Lord of your life? If so, answer, "I do."

The candidate shall respond, saying:

I do.

The minister shall then baptize the candidate, emersing him fully in the water, and saying:

Upon this public confession of your faith in the Lord Jesus Christ and your determination to leave all and follow Him, I baptize you,————— (full name of candidate), in the name of the Father, and of the Son, and of the Holy Ghost.

PRAYER

After all of the candidates have been baptized, the minister, or someone appointed by him, shall pray for those who have been baptized, committing them to God for His protection, and dedicating them to service for Christ.

The service may end with an appropriate hymn and a benediction.

—*Harry S. Garrett*

A BAPTISMAL SERVICE

Biblical Authority

"Ye have obeyed from the heart that form of doctrine which was delivered unto you." (Rom. 6:17)

The Meaning of Baptism

"I am crucified with Christ: nevertheless I live; yet not I, but Christ liveth in me: and the life which I now live in the flesh I live by the faith of the Son of God, who loved me, and gave himself for me." (Gal. 2:20)

Water baptism is a step whereby a child of God identifies himself with Christ in His death, burial, and resurrection. Crucifixion with Christ is not some particular kind of experience which we receive when we accept Christ as our Saviour. It is a substitutionary death which God credited to all mankind when His Son died on the cross. He died for the entire race. Because of this, and through faith in it, we can now become children of God. Baptism identifies us with the sacrifice by which life in Christ is made possible.

Responsibilities Assumed at Baptism

To fulfill the purpose of baptism there are five things which the candidate must do:

He must accept Christ as his personal Saviour. "But as many as received him, to them gave he power to become the sons of God." (John 1:12)

He must reckon on the fact of his death with Christ. "We thus judge, that if one died for all, then were all dead." (2 Cor. 5:14)

He must present himself for burial by baptism after he has received Christ as Saviour. "We are buried with him by baptism into death." (Rom. 6:4)

He must walk in newness of life by the power of His Spirit. "Ye are risen with him through the faith of the operation of God, who hath raised him from the dead." (Col. 2:12)

And he must daily reckon himself dead to sin, following the injunction, "Reckon ye also yourselves to be dead indeed unto sin, but alive unto God through Jesus Christ our Lord." (Rom. 6:11)

CHARGE

Before the candidate is immersed he may be charged as follows:

In presenting yourself for baptism, you desire to be identified with the gracious act of Christ whereby He died in your place; and now that you have accepted Him as your Saviour, you wish to be buried with Him by baptism. You promise by His grace and divine enabling to walk in newness of life, and thus glorify Him day by day. If this is your wish, and if you so promise, answer, "I do."

The candidate shall say:

I do.

ACT OF BAPTISM

The candidate may then be baptized, the minister saying:

On the basis of your confession of Christ as your personal Saviour, I now baptize you into fellowship with Christ in His death, so that you may rise to walk in newness of life in Him; in the name of the Father, and of the Son, and of the Holy Spirit. Amen.

—*Allan A. Swift*

A BAPTISMAL SERVICE

ADDRESS TO THE CONGREGATION

The minister, addressing the people, may say:
From apostolic times the church has regarded
baptism as an outward sign of the inward work of
grace by which a person is made a new creature in
Christ Jesus and a part of His body, the church.
It is recognized that baptism signifies that there
has previously been acceptance of the Christ as
Saviour and Lord. Let us therefore offer our praise
and gratitude to God, our Father, for these people
(this person) who, having given their (his/her)
hearts to the Lord, have (has) obeyed His command
in presenting themselves (himself/herself) for baptism. Let us pray God's richest blessing upon them
(him/her). May those who have not as yet entered
into the fullness of the Holy Spirit's power be also
baptized with the Holy Spirit. May those who have
experienced an infilling of the Spirit be baptized
into a fellowship of service for Christ.

PRAYER

*A prayer of thanksgiving for the saving grace of
the Lord, made manifest in the candidate for baptism, is appropriate.*

BIBLICAL AUTHORITY

"There was a man of the Pharisees, named Nicodemus, a ruler of the Jews: the same came to Jesus
by night, and said unto him, Rabbi, we know that
thou art a teacher come from God: for no man can

do these miracles that thou doest, except God be with him. Jesus answered and said unto him, Verily, verily, I say unto thee, Except a man be born again, he cannot see the kingdom of God. Nicodemus saith unto him, How can a man be born when he is old? can he enter the second time into his mother's womb, and be born? Jesus answered, Verily, verily, I say unto thee, Except a man be born of water and of the Spirit, he cannot enter into the kingdom of God. That which is born of the flesh is flesh; and that which is born of the Spirit is spirit. Marvel not that I said unto thee, Ye must be born again. The wind bloweth where it listeth, and thou hearest the sound thereof, but canst not tell whence it cometh, and whither it goeth: so is every one that is born of the Spirit." (John 3:1-8)

"Then Peter said unto them, Repent, and be baptized every one of you in the name of Jesus Christ for the remission of sins, and ye shall receive the gift of the Holy Ghost. For the promise is unto you, and to your children, and to all that are afar off, even as many as the Lord our God shall call. And with many other words did he testify and exhort, saying, Save yourselves from this untoward generation. Then they that gladly received his word were baptized: and the same day there were added unto them about three thousand souls. And they continued stedfastly in the apostles' doctrine and fellowship, and in the breaking of bread, and in prayers." (Acts 2:38-42)

ADDRESS TO THE CANDIDATES

You who have presented yourselves as candidates for baptism have heard this congregation give thanks for you and pray God's blessing upon your lives. It is proper now, that in the hearing of this congregation you should make known your faith in the Lord in whose name you are to be baptized.

CONFESSION OF FAITH

The minister shall question the candidates, saying:

Have you accepted Christ as your Saviour and Lord?

Each candidate shall answer:

I have.

Have you turned from every known sin?

The candidates shall answer:

I have.

Will you earnestly endeavor to live an exemplary Christian life?

The candidates shall answer:

I will.

Do you desire baptism in water commanded by our Lord as an outward testimony of your faith?

Each of the candidates shall answer:

I do.

PRAYER

The prayer may be a request for God to accept the candidates, and bless and keep them in His will and by His almighty power.

ACT OF BAPTISM

A hymn shall be sung while the candidates retire

to dressing rooms, and are made ready for entrance into the water.

The minister himself, entering the water, shall say or read:

"God commendeth his love toward us, in that, while we were yet sinners, Christ died for us. Therefore as by the offence of one judgment came upon all men to condemnation; even so by the righteousness of one the free gift came upon all men unto justification of life. Moreover the law entered, that the offence might abound. But where sin abounded, grace did much more abound: that as sin hath reigned unto death, even so might grace reign through righteousness unto eternal life through Jesus Christ our Lord."   (Rom. 5:8, 18, 20, 21)

"What shall we say then? Shall we continue in sin, that grace may abound? God forbid. How shall we, that are dead to sin, live any longer therein? Know ye not, that so many of us as were baptized into Jesus Christ were baptized into his death? Therefore we are buried with him by baptism into death: that like as Christ was raised up from the dead by the glory of the Father, even so we also should walk in newness of life. For if we have been planted together in the likeness of his death, we shall be also in the likeness of his resurrection: knowing this, that our old man is crucified with him, that the body of sin might be destroyed, that henceforth we should not serve sin. For he that is dead is freed from sin. Now if we be dead with Christ, we believe that we shall also live with him: knowing that Christ being raised from the dead dieth no more; death hath no more dominion over him. For in that he died, he died unto sin once: but in that he liveth, he liveth unto God. Likewise reckon ye also yourselves to be dead indeed unto sin, but alive unto God through Jesus Christ our Lord." (Rom. 6:1-11)

Then the candidates, entering the water one at a time, shall be immersed by the minister who shall say:

————— (full name of candidate), I baptize thee in the name of the Father, and of the Son, and of the Holy Spirit. Amen.

HYMN

Among the hymns suitable for closing are: "The Church's One Foundation," "Blest Be the Tie," "How Firm a Foundation," "The Solid Rock."

BENEDICTION

—*William E. Pickthorn*

FORMULAS

I baptize you in the name of the Father, and of the Son, and of the Holy Ghost. Amen.

Upon your confession of faith in Jesus Christ as Saviour and Lord, I baptize you,————— (full name), in the name of the Father, and of the Son, and of the Holy Spirit.

On the authority of the Lord Jesus Christ, I baptize you in the name of the Father, and of the Son, and of the Holy Ghost. Amen.

Upon your confession of Jesus Christ as your personal Saviour and your professed desire to make Him Lord of your life; I baptize you in the name of God, the Father; and of the Lord Jesus Christ, His only Son; and of the Holy Ghost, the Eternal Spirit of Promise. Amen.

Reception of Members

BIBLE REFERENCES

"O magnify the Lord with me, and let us exalt his name together." (Ps. 34:3)

"One is your Master, even Christ; and all ye are brethren." (Matt. 23:8)

"The same day there were added unto them about three thousand souls." (Acts 2:41)

"The Lord added to the church daily such as should be saved." (Acts 2:47)

"Now there were in the church that was at Antioch certain prophets and teachers; as Barnabas, and Simeon that was called Niger, and Lucius of Cyrene, and Manaen, which had been brought up with Herod the tetrarch, and Saul." (Acts 13:1)

"And when they were come, and had gathered the church together, they rehearsed all that God had done with them, and how he had opened the door of faith unto the Gentiles. And there they abode long time with the disciples." (Acts 14:27, 28)

"For as we have many members in one body, and all members have not the same office: so we, being many, are one body in Christ, and every one members one of another." (Rom. 12:4, 5)

"For as the body is one, and hath many members, and all the members of that one body, being many, are one body: so also is Christ. For by one Spirit are we all baptized into one body, whether we be Jews or Gentiles, whether we be bond or free; and have been all made to drink into one Spirit. For the body is not one member, but many. If the foot shall say, Because I am not the hand, I am not of the body; is it therefore not of the body? And if the ear shall say, Because I am not the eye, I am not of the body; is it therefore not of the body? If the whole body were an eye, where were the hearing? If the whole were hearing, where were the smelling? But now hath God set the members every one of them in the body, as it hath pleased him. And if they were all one member, where were the body? But now are they many members, yet but one body. And the eye cannot say unto the hand, I have no need of thee: nor again the head to the feet, I have no need of you. Nay, much more those members of the body, which seem to be more feeble, are necessary: and those members of the body, which we think to be less honourable, upon these we bestow more abundant honour; and our uncomely parts have more abundant comeliness. For our comely parts have no need: but God hath tempered the body together, having given more abundant honour to that part which lacked: that there should be no schism in the body; but that the members should have the same care one for another. And whether one member suffer, all the members suffer with it; or one member be honoured, all the members rejoice with it. Now ye are the body of Christ, and members in particular."

(1 Cor. 12:12-27)

"Grow up into him in all things, which is the head, even Christ: from whom the whole body fitly joined together and compacted by that which every joint supplieth, according to the effectual working in the measure of every part, maketh increase of the body unto the edifying of itself in love."

(Eph. 4:15, 16)

"We are members one of another."   (Eph. 4:25)

"For we are members of his body, of his flesh, and of his bones."   (Eph. 5:30)

"As newborn babes, desire the sincere milk of the word, that ye may grow thereby: if so be ye have tasted that the Lord is gracious. To whom coming, as unto a living stone, disallowed indeed of men, but chosen of God, and precious, ye also, as lively stones, are built up a spiritual house, an holy priesthood, to offer up spiritual sacrifices, acceptable to God by Jesus Christ."   (1 Peter 2:2-5)

RECEPTION OF MEMBERS

INTRODUCTION

The candidates shall be seated directly before the minister, who may introduce the service by reading from the Bible:

BIBLICAL AUTHORITY

"He found him in a desert land, and in the waste howling wilderness; he led him about, he instructed him, he kept him as the apple of his eye."
(Deut. 32:10)

"And the Lord their God shall save them in that day as the flock of his people: for they shall be as the stones of a crown, lifted up as an ensign upon his land." (Zech. 9:16)

"And they shall be mine, saith the Lord of hosts, in that day when I make up my jewels; and I will spare them, as a man spareth his own son that serveth him." (Mal. 3:17)

ADDRESS TO THE CONGREGATION

The minister may then address the assembled witnesses in words similar to the following:

The Scriptures teach us that the church is the household of God, the body of which Christ is the head; and that it is the design of the gospel to bring together in one all who are in Christ. The fellowship of the church is the communion that its members enjoy one with another. The ends of this fellowship

97

are the maintenance of sound doctrine and of the ordinances of Christian worship, and the exercise of that power of godly admonition and discipline which Christ has committed to His Church for the promotion of holiness. Its more particular duties are: to promote peace and unity, to bear one another's burdens, to prevent each other's stumbling, to seek the intimacy of friendly society among themselves, to continue steadfast in the faith and worship of the gospel, and to pray for and sympathize with each other. Among its privileges are: peculiar incitements to holiness from hearing God's Word and sharing in Christ's ordinances; and being placed under the watchful care of pastors; and the enjoyment of the blessings which are promised only to those who are of the household of faith. Into this holy relationship the persons before us, having been recommended hereto by the————— (approving body) of this church, come now to be admitted. We now propose, in the fear of God, to question them as to their faith and purposes, that you may know that they are proper persons to be admitted into the church.

CHARGE TO THE APPLICANTS

Addressing the applicants for admission, the minister may say:

You are come hither seeking the great privilege of union with the church which our Saviour has purchased with His own blood. We rejoice in the grace of God given unto you in that He has called you to be His followers, and that thus far you have run well. You have heard how blessed are the privileges, and how solemn are the duties of membership in Christ's church; and before you are fully admitted thereto, it is proper that you do here publicly renew your vows, confess your faith, and declare your purpose by answering the following questions.

Do you promise by the aid of the Holy Spirit to walk together in Christian love, strive for the advancement of this church for holiness and knowledge, promote its prosperity and spirituality, sustain its worship, doctrines, and discipline, and contribute cheerfully and regularly to the support of the ministry and activities of the church?

The applicants shall each answer:

I do.

The minister shall then say:

Do you also promise to strive to maintain family and personal devotion, seek the salvation of the lost, and walk circumspectly in the world avoiding the very appearance of evil and refuse to have any part in talebearing or backbiting, and seek that love that thinketh no evil?

The applicants shall each answer:

I do.

The minister shall continue:

Do you promise to watch over one another in brotherly love, to remember each other in prayer, to aid each other in distress and sickness, to be courteous and forgiving one to another even as God for Christ's sake hath forgiven you?

The applicants shall each answer:
I do.

CERTIFICATION

Then the minister, addressing the church, shall say:

Brethren, these persons have given satisfactory responses to our inquiries, I charge you now, if you know any reason why they should not be certified for membership, to declare it.

RECEPTION

No objection having been alleged, the minister shall say to the candidates:

We welcome you to the communion of the Church of Jesus Christ; and, in testimony of our Christian affection and the cordiality with which we receive you, I hereby extend to you the right hand of fellowship. May God grant that you may be a faithful and useful member of the Church militant until you are called to the fellowship of the Church triumphant, which is "without fault before the throne of God," and pray that the blessing of the Lord may be upon you always. Amen.

The pastor and the deacons shall then shake hands with each of the candidates.

—*Martin H. Heicksen*

RECEPTION OF MEMBERS

INTRODUCTION

An appropriate hymn may be sung by the choir or congregation while the candidates and members of the official board of the church come forward to a place reserved for them at the front of the church. Another possible procedure is for the candidates and the official board to take their places prior to the beginning of the service.

BIBLICAL AUTHORITY

Then shall follow the reading of an appropriate passage from the Scriptures:

"For as the body is one, and hath many members, and all the members of that one body, being many, are one body: so also is Christ. For by one Spirit are we all baptized into one body, whether we be Jews or Gentiles, whether we be bond or free; and have been all made to drink into one Spirit. For the body is not one member, but many. If the foot shall say, Because I am not the hand, I am not of the body; is it therefore not of the body? And if the ear shall say, Because I am not the eye, I am not of the body; is it therefore not of the body? If the whole body were an eye, where were the hearing? If the whole were hearing, where were the smelling? But now hath God set the members every one of them in the body, as it hath pleased him. And if they were all one member, where were the body? But now are they many members, yet but one body.

And the eye cannot say unto the hand, I have no need of thee: nor again the head to the feet, I have no need of you. Nay, much more those members of the body, which seem to be more feeble, are necessary: and those members of the body, which we think to be less honourable, upon these we bestow more abundant honour; and our uncomely parts have more abundant comeliness. For our comely parts have no need: but God hath tempered the body together, having given more abundant honour to that part which lacked: that there should be no schism in the body; but that the members should have the same care one for another. And whether one member suffer, all the members suffer with it; or one member be honoured, all the members rejoice with it. Now ye are the body of Christ, and members in particular. And God hath set some in the church, first apostles, secondarily prophets, thirdly teachers, after that miracles, then gifts of healings, helps, governments, diversities of tongues. Are all apostles? are all prophets? are all teachers? are all workers of miracles? have all gifts of healing? do all speak with tongues? do all interpret? But covet earnestly the best gifts: and yet shew I unto you a more excellent way." (1 Cor. 12:12-31)

ADDRESS TO THE CONGREGATION

The minister may now speak on the importance of the Church, or read the following:

The Church—or the ecclesia, the "called-out ones" —is a New Testament institution, divinely ordained of God. The Bible speaks of the ecclesia as including all of the redeemed of all time and all places. It also speaks of the ecclesia in terms of a local congregation. The Bible teaches that the ecclesia is the temple of God of which individuals are living stones, built up as a holy habitation for God. It is also a body, of which Christ is the head, and a family, the members of which are heirs of God and joint heirs with Jesus Christ.

We of————— (name of church) are a part of this great body, a local unit of the called-out ones who have renounced sin to take up our cross and follow Christ. We are brothers and sisters in the household of God. We are heirs of God and joint heirs with Jesus Christ.

CERTIFICATION

The fitness of the candidates shall be certified by the minister or by the officer responsible for examination of candidates for membership. The following may be read, or altered so that it applies to the situation:

These candidates before us now desire to become a part of this holy relationship. And since they have met the requirements for membership according to the constitution and bylaws of————— (name of church) , and have been recommended by the official board of this church, they do now come to be admitted as members. They shall then be entrusted with all the rights and privileges bestowed upon members of this congregation, and they cheerfully assume responsibility for the same.

RECEPTION

The minister shall ask the congregation to stand while the candidates come to form a line before him.

By prearrangement, the official board will form a semicircle behind the candidates.

Then the minister shall stand before each candidate separately and say:

We welcome and receive you,————— (name), into membership of————— (name of church), and cordially extend to you the right hand of fellowship, in the name of the Father, and of the Son, and of the Holy Spirit.

Having extended the right hand of fellowship to the candidate, the minister shall lay hands upon him and pray for him.

Each board member shall then shake hands with the candidate and congratulate him as a new member.

Appropriate music shall be played or a fellowship hymn sung while the new members return to their seats.

—H. W. Thiemann

RECEPTION OF MEMBERS

PRESENTATION TO THE CONGREGATION

At the proper place in the service the minister shall announce the reception of new members, saying:

It is our privilege to receive into the fellowship of this church————— (number) members who have been properly approved by the————— (name of board), and are now to receive the right hand of fellowship by this congregation. The deacons will please come to join me in the act of official welcome.

The deacons shall come forward and be ready to direct the new members as to where they shall stand.

After the deacons have taken their position at the front of the church, the minister shall say:

As his name is announced, each of the new members will please come forward and stand with the deacons facing the congregation.

It is suggested that the minister read the names slowly, allowing adequate time between names to permit the person to be recognized by the congregation.

When more than one member of a family is to be received, the names of the family members should be read together: father, mother, and then each child.

It is valuable for the minister to make some appreciative comment about each person as he comes forward: his spiritual life, his ministry in the church, the church from which he comes if he is a transfer member, etc.

THE MEMBERSHIP PLEDGE

After the entire group has been introduced, the minister shall ask the new members to turn and face the pulpit to be charged with, and to accept the responsibilities of membership.

Then the minister may say:

Having been led by the Spirit of God to receive the Lord Jesus Christ as your personal Saviour, and desiring fellowship with people of like precious faith, you do now in the presence of God and this assembly enter into covenant with one another as members of the body of Christ.

Do you promise by the aid of the Holy Spirit to walk together in Christian love, to strive for the advancement of this church, for holiness and knowledge, to promote its prosperity and spirituality, to sustain its worship, doctrines, and discipline, and to contribute cheerfully and regularly to the support of the ministry and activities of the church? If so, answer, "I do."

Each of the applicants shall answer:

I do.

Do you promise also to strive to maintain family and personal devotions, to seek the salvation of the lost, and to walk circumspectly in the world, avoiding the very appearance of evil, and to seek that love that thinketh no evil?

Each of the applicants shall answer:

I do.

Do you promise to watch over one another in brotherly love, to remember each other in prayer, to aid each other in distress and sickness, to be courteous and forgiving one to another, even as God for Christ's sake hath forgiven you?

Each of the applicants shall answer:

I do.

RECEPTION

The minister shall receive the persons before him into full membership, using words similar to the following:

We, therefore, as the Church of Jesus Christ and members of His body, now receive you into our fellowship and communion, recognizing that God already has added you to His Church. And we pray that the blessing of the Lord may be upon you always. Amen.

PRAYER

The congregation shall stand to join the minister in prayer of consecration and of thanksgiving for those who have been added to the fellowship.

After prayer the congregation may be seated.

THE RIGHT HAND OF FELLOWSHIP

The choir may sing, or there should be other suitable music while the pastor, (his wife), and then members of the board greet each new member with a handclasp and a personal word of welcome.

After each member has been greeted the congregation shall again stand to sing "Blest Be the Tie"

107

as the minister returns to the pulpit and the board members and new members return to their seats.

—William E. Pickthorn[1]

---

[1] The pledge used in this ceremony was written by Frank J. Lindquist.

Communion Service

BIBLE REFERENCES

"I am poured out like water, and all my bones are out of joint: my heart is like wax; it is melted in the midst of my bowels. My strength is dried up like a potsherd; and my tongue cleaveth to my jaws; and thou hast brought me into the dust of death. For dogs have compassed me: the assembly of the wicked have inclosed me: they pierced my hands and my feet. I may tell all my bones: they look and stare upon me. They part my garments among them, and cast lots upon my vesture."

(Ps. 22:14-18)

"Surely he hath borne our griefs, and carried our sorrows: yet we did esteem him stricken, smitten of God, and afflicted. But he was wounded for our transgressions, he was bruised for our iniquities: the chastisement of our peace was upon him; and with his stripes we are healed." (Isa. 53:4, 5)

"Ho, every one that thirsteth, come ye to the waters, and he that hath no money; come ye, buy, and eat; yea, come, buy wine and milk without money and without price. Wherefore do ye spend money for that which is not bread? and your labour for that which satisfieth not? hearken diligently unto me, and eat ye that which is good, and let your soul delight itself in fatness. Incline your ear, and come unto me: hear, and your soul shall live; and I will make an everlasting covenant with you, even the sure mercies of David." (Isa. 55:1-3)

"Seek ye the Lord while he may be found, call ye upon him while he is near: let the wicked forsake his way, and the unrighteous man his thoughts: and let him return unto the Lord, and he will have mercy upon him; and to our God, for he will abundantly pardon. For my thoughts are not your thoughts, neither are your ways my ways, saith the Lord. For as the heavens are higher than the earth, so are my ways higher than your ways, and my thoughts than your thoughts." (Isa. 55:6-9)

"Behold, the days come, saith the Lord, that I will make a new covenant with the house of Israel, and with the house of Judah: not according to the covenant that I made with their fathers in the day that I took them by the hand to bring them out of the land of Egypt; which my covenant they brake, although I was an husband unto them, saith the Lord: but this shall be the covenant that I will make with the house of Israel; After those days, saith the Lord, I will put my law in their inward parts, and write it in their hearts; and will be their God, and they shall be my people." (Jer. 31:31-33)

"Come unto me, all ye that labour and are heavy laden, and I will give you rest. Take my yoke upon you, and learn of me; for I am meek and lowly in heart: and ye shall find rest unto your souls. For my yoke is easy, and my burden is light."

(Matt. 11:28-30)

"Then came the day of unleavened bread, when the passover must be killed. And he sent Peter and

John, saying, Go and prepare us the passover, that we may eat. And they said unto him, Where wilt thou that we prepare? And he said unto them, Behold, when ye are entered into the city, there shall a man meet you, bearing a pitcher of water; follow him into the house where he entereth in. And ye shall say unto the goodman of the house, The Master saith unto thee, Where is the guestchamber, where I shall eat the passover with my disciples? And he shall shew you a large upper room furnished: there make ready. And they went, and found as he had said unto them: and they made ready the passover. And when the hour was come, he sat down, and the twelve apostles with him. And he said unto them, With desire have I desired to eat this passover with you before I suffer: for I say unto you, I will not any more eat thereof, until it be fulfilled in the kingdom of God. And he took the cup, and gave thanks, and said, Take this, and divide it among yourselves: for I say unto you, I will not drink of the fruit of the vine until the kingdom of God shall come. And he took bread, and gave thanks, and brake it, and gave unto them, saying, This is my body which is given for you: this do in remembrance of me. Likewise also the cup after supper, saying, This cup is the new testament in my blood, which is shed for you." (Luke 22:7-20)

"For God so loved the world, that he gave his only begotten Son, that whosoever believeth in him should not perish, but have everlasting life. For God sent not his Son into the world to condemn the world; but that the world through him might be saved. He that believeth on him is not condemned: but he that believeth not is condemned already, because he hath not believed in the name of the only begotten Son of God. And this is the condemnation, that light is come into the world, and men loved darkness rather than light, because their deeds were evil. The Father loveth the Son, and hath given all things into his hand. He that believeth on the Son hath everlasting life: and he that believeth not the Son shall not see life; but the wrath of God abideth on him." (John 3:16-19, 35, 36)

"And Jesus said unto them, I am the bread of life: he that cometh to me shall never hunger; and he that believeth on me shall never thirst. I am that bread of life. Your fathers did eat manna in the wilderness, and are dead. This is the bread which cometh down from heaven, that a man may eat thereof, and not die. I am the living bread which came down from heaven: if any man eat of this bread, he shall live for ever: and the bread that I will give is my flesh, which I will give for the life of the world." (John 6:35, 48-51)

"Then Jesus said unto them, Verily, verily, I say unto you, Except ye eat the flesh of the Son of man, and drink his blood, ye have no life in you. Whoso eateth my flesh, and drinketh my blood, hath eternal life; and I will raise him ur at the last day. For my flesh is meat indeed, and my blood is drink indeed. He that eateth my flesh, and drinketh

112

my blood, dwelleth in me, and I in him. As the living
Father hath sent me, and I live by the Father: so he
that eateth me, even he shall live by me."

(John 6:53-58)

"And upon the first day of the week, when the
disciples came together to break bread, Paul preached
unto them."   (Acts 20:7)

"And this is my covenant unto them, when I shall
take away their sins."   (Rom. 11:27)

"The cup of blessing which we bless, is it not
the communion of the blood of Christ? The bread
which we break, is it not the communion of the body
of Christ? For we being many are one bread, and one
body: for we are all partakers of that one bread."

(1 Cor. 10:16, 17)

"Ye cannot drink the cup of the Lord, and the
cup of devils: ye cannot be partakers of the Lord's
table, and of the table of devils."   (1 Cor. 10:21)

"Now of the things which we have spoken this
is the sum: We have such an high priest, who is set
on the right hand of the throne of the Majesty in
the heavens; a minister of the sanctuary, and of the
true tabernacle, which the Lord pitched, and not
man. For every high priest is ordained to offer gifts
and sacrifices: wherefore it is of necessity that this
man have somewhat also to offer. But now hath he
obtained a more excellent ministry, by how much
also he is the mediator of a better covenant, which
was established upon better promises. For if that

first covenant had been faultless, then should no place have been sought for the second. For finding fault with them, he saith, Behold, the days come, saith the Lord, when I will make a new covenant with the house of Israel and with the house of Judah. For this is the covenant that I will make with the house of Israel after those days, saith the Lord; I will put my laws into their mind, and write them in their hearts: and I will be to them a God, and they shall be to me a people."

(Heb. 8:1-3, 6, 8, 10)

"Neither by the blood of goats and calves, but by his own blood he entered in once into the holy place, having obtained eternal redemption for us. For if the blood of bulls and of goats, and the ashes of an heifer sprinkling the unclean, sanctifieth to the purifying of the flesh: how much more shall the blood of Christ, who through the eternal Spirit offered himself without spot to God, purge your conscience from dead works to serve the living God?"

(Heb. 9:12-14)

"Elect according to the foreknowledge of God the Father, through sanctification of the Spirit, unto obedience and sprinkling of the blood of Jesus Christ . . . Forasmuch as ye know that ye were not redeemed with corruptible things, as silver and gold, from your vain conversation received by tradition from your fathers; but with the precious blood of Christ, as of a lamb without blemish and without spot."

(1 Peter 1:2, 18, 19)

"From Jesus Christ, who is the faithful witness, and the first begotten of the dead, and the prince of the kings of the earth. Unto him that loved us, and washed us from our sins in his own blood, and hath made us kings and priests unto God and his Father; to him be glory and dominion for ever and ever. Amen." (Rev. 1:5, 6)

A COMMUNION SERVICE

PREPARATION OF THE TABLE

A communion table shall have been prepared in advance and placed in front of the pulpit. The bread and the "wine" of the communion, in suitable containers, shall have been placed on the table and covered with a clean white cloth.

PREPARATION FOR PARTICIPATION

At an appropriate place in the church service the pastor shall announce the communion and walk to the table where he shall stand facing the congregation. While he is still at the pulpit, or after he has taken his place at the table, he may make some such statement as follows:

It was the commandment of our Lord that His followers should continue to break bread and drink the cup of blessing just as He and His apostles had done on the eve of His crucifixion. "This do in remembrance of me," Jesus said. Today, once again we joyfully obey that command.

When the announcement has been made, deacons who have been previously appointed to serve shall come forward and stand at the communion table facing the pastor.

INVITATION

The pastor, with the aid of one of the deacons, shall carefully remove the cloth, fold it, and lay it at one end of the table.

Then the pastor shall instruct the congregation as

to who may participate. He should include in his statement the fact that we do not advocate or practice closed communion, that we are not to judge and thus do not refuse service to anyone, and that each person must answer for himself to God.

The pastor may say:

Since the Lord's supper is called in the Scriptures the communion of the body of Christ and since the body of Christ is made up of blood-washed believers without respect to religious affiliation or denomination, it is not our practice to restrict access to the Lord's table. All who have given their hearts to Christ and who acknowledge Him as Lord are invited to participate with us.

BIBLICAL AUTHORITY

As the deacons continue to stand before him, the pastor may read the following, or some other suitable passage from God's Word.

(NOTE. *For brevity or variety, this passage may be shortened to include only verses* 26-28.)

"Then one of the twelve, called Judas Iscariot, went unto the chief priests, and said unto them, What will ye give me, and I will deliver him unto you? And they covenanted with him for thirty pieces of silver. And from that time he sought opportunity to betray him. Now the first day of the feast of unleavened bread the disciples came to Jesus, saying unto him, Where wilt thou that we prepare for thee to eat the passover? And he said, Go into the city to such a man, and say unto him, The Master

118

saith, My time is at hand; I will keep the passover at thy house with my disciples. And the disciples did as Jesus had appointed them; and they made ready the passover. Now when the even was come, he sat down with the twelve. And as they did eat, he said, Verily I say unto you, that one of you shall betray me. And they were exceeding sorrowful, and began every one of them to say unto him, Lord, is it I? And he answered and said, He that dippeth his hand with me in the dish, the same shall betray me. The Son of man goeth as it is written of him: but woe unto that man by whom the Son of man is betrayed! it had been good for that man if he had not been born. Then Judas, which betrayed him, answered and said, Master, is it I? He said unto him, Thou hast said. And as they were eating, Jesus took bread, and blessed it, and brake it, and gave it to the disciples, and said, Take, eat; this is my body. And he took the cup, and gave thanks, and gave it to them, saying, Drink ye all of it; for this is my blood of the new testament, which is shed for many for the remission of sins. But I say unto you, I will not drink henceforth of this fruit of the vine, until that day when I drink it new with you in my Father's kingdom. And when they had sung an hymn, they went out into the mount of Olives."

(Matt. 26:14-30)

PRAYER

The pastor, or a person appointed by him, shall pray. The prayer should include praise or adoration, confession, petition, and thanksgiving.

The prayer time should be concluded by asking for God's blessing upon the bread and "wine." This is usually done by the pastor or by another minister.

INSTRUCTION AND DISTRIBUTION

When strangers are present in the congregation, instructions should be given as to the church's procedure in partaking of the communion. The pastor may use words of his own choosing, or he may say:

It is the practice of this church to celebrate communion as a corporate act of the body of Christ assembled in this house of worship. Therefore we ask that you hold the bread and the cup until every one has been served. Then we will partake together.

The pastor shall hand the containers of bread and "wine" to the deacons who shall follow a previously worked out pattern in serving the people.

When the deacons have completed their ministry to the congregation they shall return together, place the containers on the table, and stand facing the pastor.

If the number of deacons is small enough, the pastor shall serve the deacons, and one of the deacons shall then serve him. If the number of deacons is large two or more of the deacons shall serve the others and then serve the pastor.

After all who wish to participate have received the emblems, the pastor may read or quote the following, or some other suitable verse pertaining to the bread:

"The Lord Jesus the same night in which he was

betrayed took bread: and when he had given thanks, he brake it, and said, Take, eat: this is my body, which is broken for you: this do in remembrance of me." (1 Cor. 11:23, 24)

Then the pastor may say:

Let us eat together.

The pastor may then read or quote the following or another suitable verse pertaining to the "wine":

"After the same manner also he took the cup, when he had supped, saying, This cup is the new testament in my blood: this do ye, as oft as ye drink it, in remembrance of me." (1 Cor. 11:25)

The pastor may then say:

Let us drink together.

(NOTE. *After each act of partaking, the people should be given opportunity to praise the Lord for His presence, power, and blessing.*)

COVERING THE TABLE

After all have partaken of the emblems (unless receptacles for the cups are provided at the seats) have the deacons gather the communion cups. A chorus or hymn of thanksgiving, adoration, or praise may be sung during the gathering of the cups.

The containers (with the communion cups, if it has been necessary to gather them) shall be placed carefully on the table. Then the table shall be re-covered with the cloth.

CONCLUSION

If communion has been served before the message, continue the regular service. If communion has been at the close of a service, conclude with a benediction or other desired conclusion.

(NOTE. *Usually there is a lapse of time while the deacons are serving the congregation. Appropriate music—instrumental or vocal—in keeping with the solemn occasion, may be used to lend beauty and edification to the service.*)

The communion service should never be rushed. Give the Holy Spirit opportunity to move upon the hearts of all.

It should be a solemn, holy exercise. The pastor should encourage the people to open their hearts to ask the Lord to forgive, cleanse, fill with His Spirit; and to heal souls as well as bodies.

—L. E. Halvorson

A COMMUNION SERVICE

HYMN OF DEDICATION

At a predetermined point in the church service, or in a service set aside exclusively for the celebration of communion, the preparation for the act of communion shall begin with the singing of a hymn of dedication.

A suggested suitable song is, "I am Thine O Lord."

INTRODUCTORY BIBLICAL SENTENCE

The minister shall read a Biblical statement concerning yieldedness of heart, repentance, and confession of sin. A suggested passage follows:

"The Lord is nigh unto them that are of a broken heart; and saveth such as be of a contrite spirit. Many are the afflictions of the righteous: but the Lord delivereth him out of them all." (Ps. 34:18, 19)

PRAYER OF CONFESSION

The minister shall pray for himself and for the people confessing their common need of God. It is proper to admit failures to love, to do God's perfect will, to live as overcomers, to shine as lights in the world, to live and walk in the Spirit. Sincere thought for such a prayer may be found in many of the Psalms.

The prayer may properly be concluded with a recital by the entire congregation of the Lord's Prayer·

RESPONSIVE READING

The minister and congregation shall read responsively a Bible passage which speaks of God's mercy, His willingness to abundantly pardon and to supply all our need.

The following chapter is suggested:

MINISTER: "Who hath believed our report? and to whom is the arm of the Lord revealed?

PEOPLE: For he shall grow up before him as a tender plant, and as a root out of a dry ground: he hath no form nor comeliness; and when we shall see him, there is no beauty that we should desire him.

MINISTER: He is despised and rejected of men; a man of sorrows, and acquainted with grief: and we hid as it were our faces from him; he was despised, and we esteemed him not.

PEOPLE: Surely he hath borne our griefs, and carried our sorrows; yet we did esteem him stricken, smitten of God, and afflicted.

MINISTER: But he was wounded for our transgressions, he was bruised for our iniquities: the chastisement of our peace was upon him; and with his stripes we are healed.

PEOPLE: All we like sheep have gone astray; we have turned every one to his own way; and the Lord hath laid on him the iniquity of us all.

MINISTER: He was oppressed, and he was afflicted, yet he opened not his mouth: he is brought as a lamb to the slaughter, and as a sheep before her shearers is dumb, so he openeth not his mouth.

PEOPLE: He was taken from prison and from judgment: and who shall declare his generation? for he was cut off out of the land of the living: for the transgression of my people was he stricken.

MINISTER: And he made his grave with the wicked, and with the rich in his death; because he had done no violence, neither was any deceit in his mouth.

PEOPLE: Yet it pleased the Lord to bruise him; he hath put him to grief: when thou shalt make his soul an offering for sin, he shall see his seed, he shall prolong his days, and the pleasure of the Lord shall prosper in his hand.

MINISTER: He shall see the travail of his soul, and shall be satisfied: by his knowledge shall my righteous servant justify many; for he shall bear their iniquities.

PEOPLE: Therefore will I divide him a portion with the great, and he shall divide the spoil with the strong; because he hath poured out his soul unto death: and he was numbered with the transgressors; and he bare the sin of many, and made intercession for the transgressors." (Isa. 53:1-12)

HYMN OF WORSHIP

The natural response to forgiveness is thanksgiving, worship, praise. The people may be encouraged to offer praise to the Lord. They may worship Him in song.

Suitable choruses and hymns include: "My Wonderful Lord," "Jesus Is the Sweetest Name I Know."

BIBLICAL AUTHORITY

The minister, or someone appointed by him, shall read one of the Biblical passages relating to the institution or observance of communion:

"And the first day of unleavened bread, when they killed the passover, his disciples said unto him, Where wilt thou that we go and prepare that thou mayest eat the passover? And he sendeth forth two of his disciples, and saith unto them, Go ye into the city, and there shall meet you a man bearing a pitcher of water: follow him. And wheresoever he shall go in, say ye to the goodman of the house, The Master saith, Where is the guestchamber, where I shall eat the passover with my disciples? And he will shew you a large upper room furnished and prepared: there make ready for us. And his disciples went forth, and came into the city, and found as he had said unto them: and they made ready the passover. And in the evening he cometh with the twelve. And as they sat and did eat, Jesus said, Verily I say unto you, One of you which eateth with me shall betray me. And they began to be sorrowful, and to say unto him one by one, Is it I? and another said, Is it I? And he answered and said unto them, It is one of the twelve, that dippeth with me in the dish. The Son of man indeed goeth, as it is written of him: but woe to that man by whom the Son of man is betrayed! good were it for that man if he had never been born. And as they did eat, Jesus took bread, and blessed, and brake it, and gave to them, and said, Take, eat: this is my body. And he took the cup, and when he had given thanks, he gave it to them: and they all drank of it. And he said unto them, This is my blood of the new testament, which is shed for many. Verily I say unto you, I will drink no more of the fruit of the vine, until that day that I drink it new in the kingdom of God. And when they had sung an hymn, they went out into the mount of Olives." (Mark 14:12-26)

PRAYER OF INTERCESSION

At this point the minister shall pray for God to meet each person in a special way as he partakes of the communion. He should not pray for individuals as such, but rather for the needs of all of the people, holding them before God in compassion and asking for a manifestation of God's love.

INSTRUCTION

It may at times be advisable to tell the members of the congregation that all who have been born again are invited to participate in the communion.

The people shall be instructed to hold the bread and the cup until all have been served and prayer has been offered so that all may partake together.

DISTRIBUTION

Another minister or one of the deacons shall assist with the removal of the table covering.

The pastor or a person appointed by him shall hand the trays to the deacons who have been appointed to serve the congregation.

Worshipful music may be played or sung as the elements are distributed to the people.

When all of the congregation have been served the deacons shall return to the front to be served by the pastor who shall be served last by one of the deacons.

COMMUNION

The minister shall pray, or ask a deacon or a member of the congregation to pray, saying:

Let us give thanks for the broken body of our Lord, and then eat the bread together. ————— (name) will lead us in prayer.

After prayer the pastor may say:

Let us partake together in the name of our Lord.

In the same manner the pastor shall pray, or ask a deacon or a member of the congregation to pray, saying:

Let us give thanks for the precious blood of the Lord Jesus Christ, the seal of the covenant which makes us one in Him. ————— (name) will lead us in prayer.

After prayer the pastor may say:

Let us partake in fellowship with our crucified and risen Lord.

HYMN OF THANKSGIVING

Suggested hymns are " 'Tis So Sweet to Trust in Jesus," "I Will Praise Him," "His Name Is Wonderful."

The Doxology may be used.

PRAYER

The minister may commend the congregation to the Lord to the end that all may walk in newness of life.

BENEDICTION

One of the benedictions of the Word of God is suggested:

"The grace of our Lord Jesus Christ, and the love of God, and the communion of the Holy Ghost, be with you all. Amen."   (2 Cor. 13:14)

—*James R. Adkins*

A COMMUNION SERVICE

Following is an order of holy communion service designed to follow the sermon.

INVITATION

The following scriptural words of invitation, comfort, and exhortation may be used:

"Come unto me, all ye that labour and are heavy laden, and I will give you rest. For my yoke is easy, and my burden is light." (Matt. 11:28, 30)

"Him that cometh to me I will in no wise cast out." (John 6:37)

"For God so loved the world, that he gave his only begotten Son, that whosoever believeth in him should not perish, but have everlasting life." (John 3:16)

"This is a faithful saying, and worthy of all acceptation, that Christ Jesus came into the world to save sinners." (1 Tim. 1:15)

"Whosoever shall eat this bread, and drink this cup of the Lord, unworthily, shall be guilty of the body and blood of the Lord. But let a man examine himself, and so let him eat of that bread, and drink of that cup." (1 Cor. 11:27, 28)

"If we confess our sins, he is faithful and just to forgive us our sins, and to cleanse us from all unrighteousness." (1 John 1:9)

PRAYER OF CONFESSION

Psalm 51 is suggested as a good prayer, or as a good pattern for a prayer of confession.

HYMN OF HOLY COMMUNION

Most hymnals have hymns for holy communion classified in a topical index. In some hymnals they may be found under the heading, communion, or Lord's supper.

PASTORAL PRAYER

This shall be a prayer of consecration and blessing.

SCRIPTURAL WORDS OF INSTITUTION

The following passage, or one of the other Bible references to the institution of the holy communion, may be read:

"For I have received of the Lord that which also I delivered unto you, That the Lord Jesus the same night in which he was betrayed took bread: and when he had given thanks, he brake it, and said, Take, eat: this is my body, which is broken for you: this do in remembrance of me. After the same manner also he took the cup, when he had supped, saying, This cup is the new testament in my blood: this do ye, as oft as ye drink it, in remembrance of me." (1 Cor. 11:23-26)

PASTORAL INVITATION

Following the reading of the Biblical words of institution the pastor shall say:

You who do truly and earnestly repent of your

sins, trusting in Jesus Christ and His blood for cleansing and forgiveness, having received Him as your Saviour and Lord; and are in love with God and with your neighbors; and intend to lead a new life, following the commandments of God, and walking henceforth in His holy ways; draw near with faith and take this holy ordinance and these blessed elements to your spiritual comfort and strengthening.

DISTRIBUTION OF THE ELEMENTS

The manner of distribution of the elements will be determined by the size of the congregation and the way in which the people are seated. The elements may be taken to the members of the congregation, or the members of the congregation may come to the communion rail where they will kneel to be served.

No instruction to the congregation is necessary when the participants are permitted to partake immediately after receiving the bread and the wine.

PRAYER OF THANKSGIVING

This is a pastoral prayer in which the minister stands before God in behalf of the congregation to give thanks.

HYMN OF DEPARTURE

BENEDICTION

—David W. Plank